Other Prairie Adventure Books you will enjoy:
Sarah and the Magic Twenty-Fifth
Sarah and the Lost Friendship
Sarah and the Mystery of the Hidden Boy

SARAH
AND THE PELICAN

Margaret Epp
illustrated by Robert G. Doares

A Winner Book

VICTOR BOOKS

a division of SP Publications, Inc.
WHEATON. ILLINOIS 60187

Offices also in Fullerton. California • Whitby, Ontario, Canada • Amersham-on-the-Hill, Bucks, England

Third printing, 1980

All Scripture quotations are from the *King James Version.*

Library of Congress Catalog Card No. 76-50171
ISBN: 0-88207-476-8

VICTOR BOOKS
A division of SP Publications, Inc.
P.O. Box 1825 • Wheaton, Ill. 60187

Contents

CHAPTER 1

Harvesttime Excitement

THIS WAS SEPTEMBER. The breeze that slid over the windowsill into Braeburn school that day had a smoky smell. That was because of the forest fire up north. And it had a humming sound. That was because of the threshing machines, racing each other to harvest the crop. They could be miles away and clear out of sight, but you could hear them just the same.

The mischievous breeze sneaked over to where Sarah Naomi Scott sat. She was inking the outline of a map of Southeast Asia. The breeze riffled the page. Sarah's pen slipped. There! Look what the breeze had done—taken a big chunk out of China!

Now it was tickling Sarah's neck and tugging at her dress and hair.

Come out! Come out and play! it seemed to whisper.

Ooooh! She wished she could! Restlessly Sarah swung her bare feet, the soles just skimming along the floorboards under her desk.

All over the room other bare feet were as restless as hers. Nobody was working much. One first grader, little Stella Thatcher, was asleep! Her chubby arms were stretched out on the desk with her curly mop of red and gold hair spread all over them. Robbie, Sarah's 13-year-old-brother, looked very studious, but he was reading *Treasure Island.* In schooltime! It was all right though because that book was part of his literature this year. Imagine! Bertie Gerrick breathed through his mouth, chewing his tongue as he drew horse heads all over his slate. He drew horse heads whenever he had a chance. Johnny Siddons was busy too —popping balls of paper off the end of his ruler. One landed—plop!—right on Miss Haliday's head.

She didn't even look up from grading papers.

"Joh-nee!" The warning began on a low note and jumped to a high one. That was enough. The room settled into a restless, rustling, breathing quietness again.

Only the clock on the wall talked, gazing sternly back at Sarah:

"School's—not—o—ver. School's—not—o—ver.

Nee—dn't—think—it! Nee—dn't—think it!

Ten—more—min—utes. Ten—more—min—utes."

And so on and on. Bossy old clock!

And why did the last 10 minutes in school always drag along so? Some days they seemed about as long as an hour. Like today.

Sarah's mind could go skipping ahead though, even if her feet weren't allowed to. They sped straight home. This was an exciting time to be alive. For several reasons.

The first was Linda, Sarah's special best friend.

For almost a month now she had lived in the Scott home, ever since the day her aunt, Jane Bolton, fell down the stairs and broke her hip. Aunt Jane was mending in the Paxton hospital now. But meanwhile Sarah had a playmate every day, always there, always with exciting ideas of what they could do together.

Linda had seen so many countries. Her father was a diplomat, and she was born in Borneo—which sounded like a joke but wasn't. A few months ago she got infantile paralysis, and ever since then she had these Raggedy-Ann legs, limp and useless. But she was a lot of fun. *Once you got to know her.*

At first—well! For a while last spring when Linda arrived at her aunt's place the two girls were more like fighting cats than friends, spitting and clawing and arching their backs at one another. But not anymore.

Linda could make such surprising things. Out of scraps of cloth she sewed spiffy outfits for her dolls of many nations. She built whole villages of cardboard houses. And she used flour and salt and water to make whole families and rafts of pets to live in the houses.

So that was one reason.

The other reason was threshingtime.

For days Father and Stuart, Sarah's big brother, had been away from home now—working with the crew of Mr. Thatcher's outfit. One of these days the big monster of a machine with its shiny black wheels and banners of smoke and steam, would come pounding up the Scott lane. Nothing tickled Sarah's backbone like the whistle of a giant steamer.

Suddenly, a dismaying thought struck her. *What if the outfit arrives while I am in school?* She simply couldn't bear it if that happened!

"Map finished, Sarah?" Teacher spoke across her shoulder. Sarah jerked—and her pen skittered across the Gulf of Siam, leaving a trail where no trail belonged.

"Oh, dear!" sighed Sarah.

"Did I startle you?" Teacher said. "Too bad. But you seem to have been dreaming again. Well, time's up. No, I'm afraid you can't redo the assignment."

The messy sheet went on Teacher's pile—right over Susan Gerrick's neat, neat map.

"Put away your books," said Teacher. "Turn. Stand."

With a clatter of desks they stood in four rows—all except little Stella Thatcher. But when the school began singing, "Now the day is over—" the first grader jerked her head up. She rubbed her face with both pudgy hands and tried to stand. But she toppled right back into her seat again. She was that sleepy!

No other Thatcher was in school today, so Sarah helped Stella with her lunch pail and schoolbag. When Robbie came driving up in the rattly old school buggy, he and Sarah decided to take Stella all the way to her home. She couldn't be trusted to walk. Likely as not she would tumble right into the roadside grass, first chance she got, and go back to sleep! And *then* what would her mother do? She'd be worried sick.

But, what if the threshing outfit arrives at home, and we're not there to see it? Sarah worried.

Stella sat between them, leaning her head against Sarah's shoulder, yawning and blinking and shivering a little, and not saying a single word all the way home. Mrs. Thatcher was pleased that they had brought her. She said so, and she stuffed their pockets with fresh raisin cookies.

"I was baking them to bring to your Ma anyway, seeing the threshers are due at your house next," she said.

"Eek! When?" squealed Sarah.

"Today," Mrs. Thatcher answered. "For all I know they may be there now. Thanks again for bringing my sleepy little bunny home to me."

They didn't wait for more talk. Robbie made such a short turn, the buggy tilted, and the wheels scraped the underside of the box. Then he shook out the reins.

"Giddap! Shake a leg now, Wally," he called.

When he *had* to and when he *wanted* to Wally could shake all four of them at once. And today he did.

As they bounced along, Sarah scanned the road two miles to the west. The Thatcher steamer would likely move down that road on its way from the Siddons to the Scotts.

Because of the humming that filled the air and the whistling breeze and the rattly buggy wheels, it was useless for Sarah to try and pick out the sound of one engine approaching. All she could see for a while were the hills of the north Saskatchewan River, all blue today on account of the smoke haze. Then she saw a jet of smoke and steam! Like a banner waving in the wind!

"There it is! There it is! Oh, there it is!" she shouted.

Oh, goody! They were going to get home first.

A quarter of a mile from home Spencer, their collie, came galloping to meet them, as always. He raced beside them as they went swaying up the lane. In the yard they saw the wagon with the two horses, Prince and Captain, hitched to it—and their big sister Kathleen standing there, holding the reins.

"Well! What made you late?" she called before they came to a stop. Then, not waiting for an answer, "The

Turner threshing outfit is moving over to Aunt Jane Bolton's south 40 tomorrow. That means we'll have the crew here for dinner. Robbie, you're to—"

"The *Turner* crew?" said Sarah. "Then—then what about the *Thatchers?*"

"Hey, how about that!" crowed Robbie. "Two gangs at the same time! Forty men for dinner. Whew! How about that!"

"The *Thatchers?* Oh, no!" said Kathleen. "Father would have notified us if— There must be a mistake."

So they told her what Stella's ma had just told them, and what they had seen. The Thatcher outfit was on the move, all right, even if it was still about four miles away.

"Oh, no!" said Kathleen again. Then she whirled to run

toward the house, calling for Mother. Kathleen running! Grown-up ladies practically never ran. Ten-year-old girls could though.

With one spring Sarah cleared the buggy wheel and was on the ground. She gave Spencer only a little pat or two, then went skimming up the walk and into the kitchen. Robbie followed in about half a minute. For once everyone was slamming doors and no one was objecting. Mother was too busy cranking the handle of the telephone.

Central didn't answer! And the bell was silent. The telephone must be out of order. So no *wonder* Father hadn't been able to warn them.

"All right, all right!" Mother made hushing motions with her hands. All of them had been gabbling at once, no one really listening to anyone else. "There, that's better. Now. Let's plan—"

They had plenty of home-canned food for tonight, she said. So there was no need to panic. They could get it ready for the table in a hurry—and there would be plenty for all.

"But we'll have them all tomorrow," said Kathleen, worrying again.

"So we shall. And this means all of us will need to work together. Robbie, Kathleen has the wagon waiting. You'll have to go to Aunt Jane's place to see if the granary bins are all ready. I believe your father said they were, but you'd better check. I'm sure Mr. Heathe will be glad to lend a hand. And then you'll milk Aunt Jane's cows tonight. Now no protests, young man! Kathleen and I will have our hands full. And as for you, Sarah Naomi, you'll have to go to town—"

"To Blakely? *Alone?*" Sarah gasped.

"You've done it before," her mother said.

She had—once. On the very day that Aunt Jane fell downstairs and broke her hip. Sarah was the one who found her. Linda was crouching on the floor beside her, unable to get to the telephone because it was too high on the wall.

That time she had gone to Blakely to get some repairs for Father. But this time she was to buy groceries, and the brown paper shopping list was almost a yard long!

"You and Wally will have to hurry to get there before the store closes," she told Sarah. "Now, Kathleen, let's plan supper."

Sarah ran quickly to peek into the living room at Linda.

"See you later. Gotta go to town," she called importantly, waving the shopping list.

Wally was tethered to a fence post. He didn't like the idea at all when she urged him from the yard, and headed him west again. Blakely was southeast of their home. But because of the winding creek that skirted the lower end of the Scott pasture, she had to go west first, then head south, then east. Wally clip-clopped along in a discouraged sort of way. They were just about to pass the Slocum driveway when Sarah had a daring idea.

Now, not all of her ideas turned out to be good ones. Sometimes they tossed her into a pool of trouble up to her ears. But this one—well, it *seemed* right. Mrs. Slocum, with her flyaway hair and booming voice, had a heart as big as the world—that's what Mother always said. And the Slocums had a Ford touring car!

"Why, honey," shouted Mrs. Slocum, after Sarah had

explained the situation, "you did exactly the right thing. Look, this is what we'll do. You and me'll breeze to town, and we'll get those — — —   — — — groceries. (Sometimes Mrs. Slocum used words that were never spoken in the Scott home.) And then we'll breeze around the countryside, and get organized. Your ma needs a helping hand, and she's gonna get it—or my name's not Mabel Slocum. So tie up your horse, and hop in the flivver. I'll be right out."

So the two of them breezed, Sarah grinning all the way. It wasn't every day she could go scooting along at 35 miles an hour! She was making Mrs. Slocum happy too by letting her help. And in Jensen's store the big lady pushed through the shopping pretty smartly. Mr. Jensen was slowing down, he was so old. And he loved to gab with his customers. Today Mrs. Slocum never let him forget that this was a rush order.

But—she was *changing* a lot of the items!

It worried Sarah. Father wasn't as rich as some people.

"Pork-and-beans—hmmmmmm—six large tins? Make it a dozen, Ralph. A box of apples—you better make that two—" So it went.

Two boxes of prune plums. Two pounds of shredded coconut. Two pounds of shelled walnuts. Five pounds of sharp cheddar. A hundred pounds of sugar. Two hundred pounds of flour. The way they were going, the back of the car would be stuffed clear to the roof!

Six dozen white china cups and saucers—a half-dozen lamp globes—matches—two lanterns—new wicks for all the lamps—five gallons of coal oil—cornflakes, a dozen boxes at once! Yards of oilcloth for the long tables they would need. (But where would they put the tables? There wasn't room in all the Scott house for 40 men at once!)

"What's your ma doing for meat?" asked Mrs. Slocum suddenly.

"She and Kathleen were going to butcher some chickens," said Sarah.

"Add two hams—the biggest you got, Ralph," said Mrs. Slocum, just like that!

And that wasn't all. When the order was totaled up, she took out her handbag and paid for it, every last cent, herself.

"But—" began Sarah nervously.

"Now never you mind," boomed Mrs. Slocum. "Your pa and ma took on their share of neighborly work when they offered to chore for Jane Bolton. Been doin' it a month now. Time the rest of us got in on the deal."

Breezing home was more fun still. They stopped for about five minutes at each place along the way. Mrs. Slocum was organizing now. At almost every place the lady promised to do some cooking or baking, or to come and help for a half day or so.

In spite of the excitement, Sarah had a tiny bit of a sorry feeling though. She was going to miss the arrival of the steamer. But then, it wasn't every day she got to ride in a Ford touring car!

CHAPTER 2

Reluctant Cowgirl

WHEN MRS. SLOCUM and Sarah chugged past Aunt Jane Bolton's driveway, Robbie was just letting the cows out of the barn. Next he'd have to run the milk through the cream separator, rinse the machine, and carry the cream to the icehouse to cool. Then he'd have to feed the calves—

So Robbie was missing the excitement at home too. And he didn't even have the fun of this car ride. Poor Robbie. Of all the jobs on a farm, he thought milking cows was the very worst. That was girls' work, he said.

At the Slocum driveway Sarah climbed down and went pelting up the lane to get Wally and the buggy. Mrs. Slocum breezed on to the Scott's with the groceries and things.

Sarah listened for the sound of the steamer. Home was a half mile from here. She should be able to hear the giant engine clearly. But her heart was pounding from the run and the excitement. Perhaps that was why she couldn't hear anything else.

Wally ran willingly enough now. And Spencer recognized the beat of his hooves and the rattle of the wheels, so he came flying—yipping and waving his plumelike tail. But Sarah could see home now. She could see clear to the creek and the crumbling old strawstack. That's where the threshing outfit ought to be lined up. But it wasn't.

A funny sinking feeling came over her. Supposing this was all a *mistake*— Supposing Mrs. Thatcher had misunderstood— Or supposing she and Robbie had misunderstood her— Supposing Mrs. Slocum had gone and organized all that help and no machine was coming! Not for *days*, maybe!

Sarah's fingers shook when she unhitched Wally and turned him into the pasture. Mrs. Slocum's car stood near the garden gate. The groceries were still there—the whole mountain of them. Sarah's heart skittered lower still. She raced past the car and up the walk. In a minute now she would know.

Just inside the entry she stood still, listening, not breathing—

"And don't you worry none, Sheila Scott," came Mrs. Slocum's big voice. "Everythin's under control."

"Well, it's very kind—" began Mother.

"What we've got to decide is this—would it be easier to cook for one gang of 40, or for two gangs of 20 each?" said Mrs. Slocum.

Sarah's breath left with a happy *whoosh*. No mistake. The steamer was coming. But why hadn't it come yet? She slid into the kitchen, the linoleum cool and smooth under her feet.

"Some ladies," Mrs. Slocum was saying, "sort of thought

maybe you'd want them to cook for the Turner gang over in Jane Bolton's kitchen—"

A thinking sort of silence settled over the room. Sarah pinched a tiny bit of cooky dough and nibbled it. She could just about guess how Mother's thoughts were running.

It would be easier if only one crew came here. But Aunt Jane was sort of particular with her place. Other ladies might not be. She'd feel bad if it got messed up.

"N-no," said Mother. "I think we can manage here. We've decided to put up trestle tables outdoors—and hope for pleasant weather. We'll serve dinner and supper out there for all, breakfast indoors for the Thatcher crew, and we'll send breakfast over to the machine for the Turner crew. It's so kind of all you la—" That minute she noticed Sarah. "Well, Sarah! So you thought it time for one of your Sarah-to-the-rescue stunts, did you?" Mother didn't sound displeased though. "Better get washed and have your supper before the machine arrives."

"What hap—" began Sarah.

"That child's got a good head on her shoulders," said Mrs. Slocum in a loud whisper.

It made her feel so good, Sarah forgot to ask why the machine was delayed. The main thing was that it hadn't come while she was gone!

Linda hadn't had her supper at the usual time, so they ate together now. Not at the usual table. A dozen naked chickens lay in a heap there. They ate at the kitchen cabinet with the breadboard pulled all the way out. It was fun. Linda wanted to know all about the trip to town. And she asked questions about threshingtime.

"It—it sounds exciting—and—and sort of *together*," Linda said. "I mean, all of you working, sort of for each other. Important work. I guess farming is like that. A family sort of thing."

And that's just exactly what it is, thought Sarah proudly, as she took a half-moon out of a raisin cooky.

Right now there were jobs waiting to be done. The reason the steamer hadn't arrived was that it stopped on the way to thresh a patch of oats for Mr. Siddons. When that was done, the machine would be on the move again —and the men were going to be here for supper.

Robbie came home just as Sarah and Linda finished eating. He dropped an apple into his pocket. And he slapped together two big sandwiches, bread with thick slices of fried ham between. Then he went to help Kathleen set up the long tables, chewing as he worked. The tables stood between the clothesline and the spruce grove. That way when the sun was hot they would be in the shade, and after nightfall they could tie lanterns to the clothesline.

It was Sarah's job to fill the lanterns with oil, clean the globes, and put in the new wicks and trim them. Just when she had strung up the last lantern, Mr. Heathe came driving up the lane with a large old cookstove sitting alone in the middle of a hayrack! With Robbie and Kathleen to help him, he set it down not far from the tables. Sarah thought it looked funny there, sort of squatting, with a tall lonesome stovepipe sticking straight up.

Robbie wheeled a barrowload of chopped wood for the fire. Then he and Sarah filled a big boiler with water from the well. That was for coffee and tea and for dishwashing.

Now! Except for the food, they were ready— Oops! Not

quite. Sarah had almost forgotten. She was to drag the old bench from Father's smithy over to the porch, and place the washbasins on it. Then she must hang some towels over the railing. That was where the threshers would wash their hands. This way they needn't step indoors at all, and the ladies would have more room.

Every few minutes now a car or buggy came up the lane. Some ladies brought food into the house. Others would stay and help.

The sun had set. Night was really dropping down now.

"She's coming!" yipped Robbie.

Instantly Sarah knew who "she" was. Not another helpful neighbor. This must be the steam engine.

She followed Robbie's voice and running footsteps. To the ladder behind the barn—up the rungs that pressed the soles of her feet—onto the rough but friendly shingled roof. This was their favorite lookout.

A thin streak of light still glowed in the west. Horse hooves pounding, chains clinking, hayracks rattling, men shouting to one another—that was the crew coming on the run. Men and horses were hungry after a long day's work. But behind them came the steady thudding beat that matched the beat of Sarah's heart. Now she could see the big black shadow creeping closer along the pencil line of light.

Whoooooooeeeeee! The whistle opened wide, making Sarah jump though she had been waiting to hear it. The sound almost made her deaf, but it sent delicious shivers racing up and down her back too.

Turning the corner now—coming up the lane, growing bigger every second—Father going to meet them. You could tell where he was by the lantern that swung from his hand.

Threshingtime was here. It really was. And this year it was going to be twice as exciting as usual.

It wasn't until Sarah skipped back into the lighted kitchen that she remembered Linda again. It must be awful to be left out of all the fun. But the living room door was shut. Mother said Linda had gone to bed on the couch as usual. It might be best for Sarah to go up to her bed too.

Mother didn't insist though. It was fun to help pass platters and bowls full of food through the open window. And to watch Kathleen moving about, pouring coffee and tea, and Mrs. Darnley heaping the platters with more food at the stove.

Light from the swaying lanterns, sort of reddish, washed over the 20 faces around the trestle table—long faces, round faces, squarish ones, most of them with dust shadows around their eyes and noses. The round face with the blond cowlick belonged to Herbie Gerrick. Kathleen leaned over his shoulder now, and said something—and they were laughing together. In a few weeks they would be married and go off to California!

Herbie was going to be a preacher. He didn't look much like it, with bits of chaff in his hair and dust all over his overalls!

All the men were eating and talking, telling jokes and laughing. Tomorrow night there'd be 40 of them.

Sarah had meant to be up for breakfast at 5 o'clock. She slept till seven.

Linda Bolton was still asleep. So Sarah hurried through breakfast. She had a heaping bowlful of cornflakes! You almost never got to taste them at this house. The fried potatoes were cold, so she didn't have any of them. But she took a big slice of fresh coffee cake, with spicy juicy apples and sugary crumbs all over the top.

Then she went out to meet the morning.

Each year at threshingtime, she did the same thing before leaving for school. She would run down to the creek, skirting the big engine with its shiny wheels flying, and she'd go to the wagon box. She'd clamber over the big wheel and stand teetering on the narrow step. From up there she could hear everything and see just about everything.

She could see the hayracks moving over the wide fields, stopping at stook* after stook, picking up the sheaves of wheat. And she could see the loaded racks coming down the hill and pulling up to the separator, two by two. And the men dropping bundles onto the moving belt. And the separator chomping the sheaves, to send the rustling wheat down a spout into the wagon, and to blow the straw onto the growing pile.

She could hear the engine tootling for water, or for the racks to come hurrying with more sheaves. But—and this was the magic secret thing—if she closed her eyes, the men and horses, the racks and machines, all disappeared. Instead she could hear music playing! A hundred fiddles —and a dozen drums—and about twenty-five guitars and mandolins.

Sarah stood clutching the rim of the wagon box with both hands. The ribbon of steel that ran along the top of the box lay cool and smooth under her palms. But she was

---

*Shock or stack of sheaves

far away, sort of floating on a cloud, listening to music. Her eyes closed, she swayed in time to it. Like a sloughful of grasses sways when the wind ripples over it.

Suddenly she started. Her eyes flew open. Two hands— clutching at her ankles— Eek!

She glanced back and downward.

Father! He stood smiling up at her. His lips were moving, but she couldn't hear a word he was saying.

Then he held up his arms. Giggling she let herself fall backward into them. A swoop, almost to the ground! But he had her safe. He set her on her feet and led her a distance away from the noisy machinery.

He had news for her. She was to miss school that day. (Oh, goody!) And she was to herd the cattle—

Herd cattle!

"Ours and Aunt Jane's," said Father matter-of-factly. Just as if this was a proper threshingtime chore for a girl. "Fences will be down today, at both places. And we cannot risk the cows getting into the grain."

"But—*Father!*" she wailed.

"I know Robbie has taken care of this job other years," Father told her. "But he's needed elsewhere today. And you are quite capable of it, I know. I'm counting on you, Princess."

"But—but—Father!"

"No more buts, please, Sarah."

Something came over Sarah. "I—won't—do—it!"

She was shocked to hear the words. And Father, who had begun walking away, spun to face her.

"What was *that* I heard?"

You simply didn't say, "I won't." Not to Father. Sarah

didn't repeat it. But she still felt the same, and perhaps her face still had the *I won't* look.

"No more nonsense now. Understand?" said Father sternly.

She understood all right. Instead of being in the middle of everything, a part of the excitement, she had to chase silly old cows across a half mile of stubble to the pasture! A little while later Robbie brought Aunt Jane's herd too.

Eighteen cows altogether, and a dozen yearlings, and fifteen calves. And one unhappy cowgirl.

Actually the pasture was a very pleasant place. The winding creek was wide and shallow here, with plenty of deep grass and wild flowers on the banks. Yellow-winged blackbirds whistled as they swung on the bulrushes that crowded the marshy spots. Rolling hills sloped gently toward the creek. The grass covering them was laced with bright orange prairie lilies and bronze sunflowers and purple asters blowing in the breeze. Poplars stood in clusters here and there.

This was a favorite place on happy days. And herding cows really was a just-right job when Sarah had a lot of thinking to do. All she heard, usually, was the *turf-turf-turf* of cattle cropping the grass. And, perhaps, the lonesome caw-caw of a crow, or the bubbling song of a meadowlark.

But not today. A huge steamer a half mile north of her—and a thumping, clumping oil-pull outfit a half mile south of her— How was Sarah supposed to hear anything else?

Even Spencer had deserted her. After he helped chase the cows here he licked her hands briefly and went trotting away, his tongue lolling, his tail waving with excitement.

She was left alone—with a host of hot feelings boiling inside her.

The cows had begun to climb the hills on both sides of the creek.

"Get back, you!" she yelled.

From the hilltop she could *see* things—but if she couldn't be right there where things were happening, she didn't want to be reminded of what she was missing.

So she marched up the hill, careful not to look any distance at all. Straight to the salt lick she went. A shove—and she had started the block rolling down the slope. There. That would help keep the cattle close to the water.

Then she threw herself on the grass to brood darkly over all the reasons why she had a right to be miserable today.

Father was unfair to send her here with only cattle for company. Maybe she'd run away— Two tears trickled into the grass, startling a couple of ants. Any other time she would have giggled to see how they scurried away from the salty bath. Not today. There was no room for anything except her unhappiness.

She would run away—*then* they'd be sorry. Like about Keith—

When she was four years old her handsome big brother left home. He got mad at Father one day and slammed out of the house! No one had heard from him since.

Every day Father prayed for "our absent loved one," sounding sorry and sad.

Well, he'd be sorry too when she was gone!

CHAPTER 3

When Linda Understands

SARAH COULD TELL by the sun when dinnertime came. She had another sign too. A whole hayrackful of men, the Turner crew, drove across the pasture on their way to the Scott yard to dinner. Some stood. Some sat, dangling their legs. They came down one slope, splashed across the shallow creek, and climbed the other slope. They laughed. And they yodeled. And they talked, shouting at one another. Then the noisy load was over the hill and out of sight.

Both threshing machines were standing idle now. This was the noon hour. Only the separator tenders would still be at work, clambering over the big machines, dropping some oil in all the right places with their long-necked oilcans, so the wheels and cogs would run well this afternoon.

But Sarah thought of the others—the 40 men who would be crowding the long, shady table outdoors. And the women who would be carrying fried chicken and mashed potatoes and gravy, and creamed vegetables, and sliced ham, and salads, and pies— It would have been such fun to help.

Most likely, everyone would be too busy to remember one little cowgirl alone here in the meadow with a lot of stupid cattle.

A sound made her raise her head. A car coming. Across the *field?* Its snort grew louder by the minute. And, sure enough, Herbie Gerrick's runabout came jiggling and rocking down the hill! It stopped a few feet away from her.

"Dinner!" called Herbie, grinning cheerfully at her. "Who's hungry?"

He hopped out and came carrying a four-gallon milk pail! A clean tea towel covered the top.

"Your tablecloth, ma'am," said Herbie. He whipped it off, and spread it on the grass for her.

First came a heavy mixing bowl containing all the hot things—chicken, and oh, everything! Under that, wrapped in newspaper, was another bowl with the cold things— salads, pickles, and a blueberry pie baked in an enamel saucer. A pint jar of cold milk was included too.

But Sarah couldn't start eating. Somehow a big marble had got stuck in her throat.

Herbie had left to take dinner to the machineman over at Aunt Jane's place.

Sarah was alone. She noticed a note tucked between the pie and the milk. From Linda!

Mostly the sheet was covered with funny little drawings. One was a thin girl with rag-doll legs perched on the tip of a tree. "Keeping out of everybody's way," it said. Underneath the tree, plump ladies were running with platters of food—behind men who were running with pitch-forks in their hands! A dog was chasing a cat that was chasing a skinny chicken. Another drawing pictured a girl with dark pigtails, riding a frisky calf. She was yelling, "Stop! I want to get off!"

Sarah giggled. But suddenly the ache in her throat was too much. Before she knew it, she was sobbing into the grass, her dinner completely forgotten. That's the way Herbie found her a few minutes later.

She hadn't heard his runabout returning. She was too busy thinking sad and sorry thoughts.

Of Linda, who couldn't walk at all, but who could make a joke of her dangling legs. And Linda wasn't even a Christian. At least, not as far as Sarah knew. Sometimes Sarah had talked to her friend about the day *she* became a Christian. In a quiet way it seemed as if Linda was eager to hear about it, but she never said she wanted to become a Christian too.

And now, Sarah wondered sadly, would she ever be able to talk to Linda about it again? Or would she be ashamed to? She hadn't acted like a Christian this morning. She still didn't feel like one. The way she was so angry with Father—and the way she sassed back to him— Why, she'd never done it before! At least, not since that day in July when he helped her understand about giving herself to Jesus.

"Mind telling me what's wrong?" Herbie asked.

Somehow, Sarah wasn't startled or surprised to find Herbie there beside her. After a bit he shoved his bandana under the crook of her arm. It was clean, though it smelled of chaff and oil and Herbie Sarah sat up and blew her nose and mopped her face.

Then they talked.

A few times before, this past summer, he had helped Sarah when she was in trouble. Some people at Braeburn thought it a joke that a chubby young farmer wanted to go away to school because he thought God wanted him to be a preacher. Sarah knew he was going to be a wonderful one.

Some of the things they talked about today were things she would never say to anyone else. But he helped her. Most of all he helped her see that God doesn't stop loving you when you do wrong. And that the moment you are sorry and tell Him so, He forgives.

"But—" said Sarah in a small voice, "what about Father?"

"He's your father still, isn't he? He'll understand. You wait and see." Herbie rose and stretched his arms, looking a bit tired. "Now you'd better eat your dinner—and I'd better go eat mine."

When he left, Sarah repacked the pail and carried it to the top of the hill. The machines had begun humming again. From the hilltop she could watch the cattle to make sure they did not stray far. She could see the two crews sort of racing as they threshed the crop. She leaned her back against the rough bark of the poplar tree, and slowly she ate the good things Mother had sent her.

After a long lazy while, Herbie's runabout came jouncing across the field again! So then Sarah knew it must be lunchtime [snacktime]—4 o'clock. The car looked pretty crowded. Sarah could see that a couple of ladies were with

Herbie. A moment later she recognized Kathleen and Mrs. Darnley.

The women held boxes and pails on their laps—sandwiches and cookies and things. They ought to be in the rumble seat! There was room for them. But when the runabout drew near, she saw Linda Bolton and Susan Gerrick sitting in the rumble seat! They had come to keep her company.

Herbie carried Linda to the foot of the tree beside Sarah. Kathleen arranged some blankets and pillows for her. Then the three girls were left to themselves.

For just a tiny minute Sarah was sorry to see Susan. She and Herbie's little sister were pretty good friends. But not as close as she and Linda. They didn't need anyone else there to have a good time. They could always think up interesting story games to play.

Susan—well, she had hardly any imagination at all. Her ma always bragged on her a lot because she was so capable. *Capable* meant mopping floors and dusting furniture just as thoroughly as her ma could. That's what Mrs. Gerrick said! And it meant milking a cow every evening, and changing sheets and pillowcases on all the beds on Saturdays, and every so often it meant baking a cake—all by herself.

Susan was only 10, almost two months younger than Sarah!

But, she never read a storybook unless she had to! She never could pretend that she was Alice in Wonderland, or the Lady Rowena, or Meg March—or anybody.

"Why?" she would ask, looking puzzled and a bit unhappy. "I'm Susan Gerrick."

But today she ran about quite cheerfully, collecting rocks and ferns and things so Sarah and Linda could build a farmyard under the poplar trees on the hill.

They made roads of earth and buildings of sticks. They scooped out a winding creek and built a bridge over it. They plaited a windbreak of leafy twigs. The farm looked splendid.

Then Susan came with a handful of smooth white pebbles. "They look sort of like sheep. *Sort* of," she said, almost timidly. As if she expected Sarah to contradict her.

But they did—they really did. Sarah scattered the pebbles over the make-believe pasture. Susan sat on her heels, studying the effect with satisfaction.

"I like sheep best of all animals," she said.

Whooo! *Sheep!* Sarah thought of Spencer the collie—and Ginger the cat—and of Prince and Captain, their Sunday-go-to-meeting team of horses. Why, all four of them were her *friends*. They were glad whenever they saw her coming—and sorry to see her go. *Sheep.*

"On account of the Bible," added Susan softly.

So then Sarah was glad she had kept her thoughts to herself. "The Bible does have lovely things to say about sheep," Sarah said. "Some sad things too. Like 'All we like sheep have gone astray. . . .' And 'As a sheep before her shearers is dumb, so He openeth not His mouth. . . .' That verse tells about the Lord Jesus. People dared to tell the meanest lies about Him—and He *let* them. He just let them. He never tried to defend Himself. And so, at last, they crucified Him."

"There is a sheep verse that tells about that too," Susan said, " 'I am the Good Shepherd: the Good Shepherd giveth His life for the sheep.' "

"That sounds like an exciting story. Tell it!" begged Linda.

It was a funny thing. Sarah had told her about the Lord Jesus before—about His death on the cross and all. And each time Linda had looked as if she was interested, maybe. But she didn't seem to think it had a thing to do with Linda Bolton.

Now in a hushed voice Susan was telling the same story —the very same. Somehow the white pebbles on the little pasture made it so real. There was the flock. And here was the Shepherd. And there was a runaway sheep. (Who said Susan didn't have any imagination?) And there, creeping out of the woods, came the wicked robber—a wolf, maybe, or a lion, or a bear. He meant to have the runaway sheep. But the Shepherd saw the danger, and He fought off the robber—*and He got killed.* But the sheep was safe.

"The Shepherd is Jesus, you know," said Susan. "When He died on the cross it was because of our sins. Yours too, Linda."

Sarah hardly dared to breathe. But she was praying in her heart. *Oh, dear Lord Jesus, help Linda to see!* Her hand trembled a little as she patted the tiny bridge into shape.

Linda's face had a sober, wistful look. The lovely blue eyes had a faraway expression. She seemed to be staring only at the Turner machine a half mile away. Then she turned to Susan.

"Tell me how," she said.

"You mean—how to be a Christian?" Susan said.

It's a funny thing. You want something to happen—oh, so much! And you pray for it to happen. And when it does happen you don't really believe it.

"You really mean it?" said Susan.

"Really," said Linda.

Maybe Susan didn't have much imagination. But she knew why the Lord Jesus came into the world—and why He died—and about how He rose again to live forevermore! And how you can invite Him to come and live in your heart.

The poplar trees rustled. And there was the *turf-turf-turf* of cattle cropping grass. And to the north and south there were the hum and toot and rattle of two machines threshing grain. But the only sound that seemed to matter now was Linda's voice. It shook a bit. Linda was asking the Lord Jesus to cleanse her and to live in her for always.

So the day that began sadly for Sarah turned into one of the happiest days of all. Linda was a Christian now. The three of them could talk about the Lord Jesus, loving Him, and loving each other, as they worked away at their make-believe farm on the hill.

Sarah thought of something else, something really thrilling. There's a Bible verse that says that if two or three Christians agree to pray about a thing, God will answer. Well, now there were three of them. So they could really pray that God would heal Linda's legs.

"Sure, I'll pray," agreed Susan, nodding. "But Ma always says we got to help answer our prayers too. Couldn't you exercise your legs a bit? When I had scarlet fever I was in bed almost three weeks. My legs got wobbly as anything. That's because I hadn't used them. You got to exer— Hey! You! Robbie Scott!"

Sarah's brother and Spencer had sneaked up on them! With a shrill whistle Robbie suddenly jumped out from behind the tree trunks. He had brought the wheelbarrow with him. He dropped the handles.

"Your chariot, ma'am!" he said grandly to Linda.

Then he and Spencer raced down the slope to the creek. He helped the collie round up the Scott cattle and start them homeward—and then he began chasing Aunt Jane's cattle southward. Susan and Sarah tugged and lifted Linda into the barrow. Then, Susan pulling and Sarah pushing, they trundled her along the winding cowpath for home.

But Spencer's plumelike tail was ahead of them all the way. They reached the corner of the garden fence just as he nudged the last calf into the corral and Kathleen dropped the bars into place to shut the cattle safely in for night.

After all the excitement and fresh air, Linda went straight to bed. She had her supper on a tray tonight. Susan left immediately too. Her mother whisked her home, because they had their chores to do too.

"Hadn't you better eat early and go to bed?" Mother suggested.

The idea was tempting. Sarah almost did it.

She needn't go to sleep right away. She could watch most of the excitement from the upstairs window— The threshers unhitching their teams and watering them at the trough—about 30 horses snorting and slurping and shaking their tired shoulders— And the lanterns swinging on the clothesline—and the long tables filling up with threshers. And she wouldn't have to meet Father.

By tomorrow, maybe, he would have forgotten. Maybe. Maybe it would seem as if it had never really happened at all.

Sarah felt as if she had been in a far country, just like the runaway boy in the Bible. She had asked Jesus to forgive her. Father didn't know that though. Maybe he would forget—but she wouldn't feel really comfortable until he knew that she was sorry.

"Please, Mother, mayn't I help?" she asked.

"Oh—all right," her mother agreed.

She brought a barrowload of wood to the outdoor cookstove. She scrubbed the washbasins and hung clean towels over the porch railing. She washed her hands, then carried bowlfuls of dills and saucerfuls of butter and placed them here and there along the tables. Then she stood for a while in the damp cool grass, watching the sparks that flew from the lonesome-looking smokestack.

That's where Mother found her.

"Eat your supper, wash your feet, and go to bed," said Mother. There was no "hadn't you better" in her voice this time. "You'll be unfit for school tomorrow otherwise."

"Won't I herd cows tomorrow?"

"No, they've cleared the east 40, so the fence can be restrung. Now no more dawdling."

So Sarah had her supper at the corner of the kitchen cabinet again. Then she took a basinful of warm water and sat on the porch to wash her feet. The water felt good, but she didn't have much time to twiddle her toes in it. Because, that minute—*Whoooooeeee!* The throttle of the steam engine opened wide. They were quitting for the night.

The engine stood still. How startlingly quiet the night seemed! But teamsters were coming up the hill and beginning to unhitch. Hurry, hurry, hurry, Sarah Naomi!

Just as she sloshed the water into the grass she heard clumping boots on the walk. Father's. And she sat there wiping her feet, just where the light from the window fell on the porch! She couldn't hide now if she had wanted to.

Father wasn't alone though.

"Well, Miss Sarah Naomi," came Mr. Slocum's teasing voice, "and where've *you* been all day? Herding cows? You don't say! You're Pa's right-hand man, I shouldn't wonder." And he laughed that high tee-hee-hee laugh of his.

"Couldn't manage without her," said Father firmly.

He gave her a hand up. That moment someone moved

the lamp from the window. In the dark Sarah stooped quickly to kiss the back of Father's hand. Prickly—salty—the hand was still for an instant. Then it moved to the top of her head and rubbed her hair gently.

Father knew. She didn't need words. He knew—and he loved her.

"No, I couldn't do without my princess," he said aloud. "Had your supper yet? Good. It's late. Better scamper up to bed."

"Yes, Father. Good night!" she said.

She felt as if she could fly up the dark stairs. She had been in a far country. Oh, many sad and lonesome miles away. But she was *home* now.

CHAPTER 4

One by One, and Two by Two

SARAH HAD HOPED the threshers would still be there when she got home from school. Wally was trotting along in that businesslike way he sometimes had—his head hanging low, as if he had to watch the trail very carefully so as not to stumble. He was really covering ground today.

But before they reached the Darnley corner Sarah could see a line of hayracks rattling away westward. So then she knew. And that very moment she heard the high triumphant shriek of the steam engine.

Finished, it said. *All through here!*

Home was a half mile north and a half mile east of here. Across the field she could see the house and the barn—and puffs of smoke and steam rising between them now. The threshing outfit must be lumbering up the slope from the creek.

"Giddap!" she called, and she shook out the reins.

Wally and the steam engine met about an eighth of a mile from home. But Wally politely gave the whole road to the puffing, chuffing monster. He didn't like steam engines nearly as much as Sarah did. In fact, he crowded the wheels of the buggy right against the barbed wire fence, and stood there, snorting impatiently.

In his high cab, Mr. Thatcher showed his teeth in a wide smile. He didn't open the throttle. Wally looked as if he might have taken off like a startled jackrabbit. So all Mr. Thatcher and his separator tender did was to swing their greasy caps in greeting.

Sarah watched the outfit crawl past, then soberly she and Wally trotted home.

There was an empty *nothing* sort of feeling in the yard. This was odd. Because the yard was *full*. In the background, near the creek, was the big new straw pile, looking like a mountain almost. Here the cows crowded around the trough, and Spencer trotted importantly around the fringe, to make sure no cow took it into her head to start for the pasture again. Robbie headed them toward the barn just as Kathleen came from the house with about five empty milk pails clanking on her arms.

Threshingtime was over. That was what gave Sarah the empty feeling. The fields were bare as anything with all the stooks gone. Tables, benches, lanterns and cookstove had disappeared from the yard.

The Turner crew had expected to finish at Aunt Jane's at noon today, Sarah knew. So they wouldn't be back here for supper. Father and Stuart must have gone too. They belonged to the regular Thatcher crew.

Sarah unharnessed Wally, turned him into the pasture, and tossed a bundle of oats over the bars. Then she raced for the house.

"Mother!" she called, dropping her lunch pail onto the kitchen table.

It clanged hollowly. And somehow Sarah knew then—even before Linda's answer came. The house always seemed to have a peculiar throbbing feeling when Mother was away.

"Hello! Aunt Sheila's gone to help at the Slocums," called Linda. "Come, look what I've made."

Of course Mother would have gone. Neighbors helped one another. That's the way it ought to be. But Sarah felt dismal—even when Linda showed her a nifty new doll outfit. Gay snippets of cloth were scattered over the couch and floor. And the Austrian *Bergmaedel* (mountain girl) looked charming in her bright skirt and blouse.

Linda was awfully clever. She had about 24 dolls of many nations finished now. She made the dolls as well as their clothes, which seemed almost like magic to Sarah. Linda held up her *Bergmaedel* now, twirling it slowly, looking at it critically.

"Next, I'm going to make Kathleen—in her wedding things, you know," she said happily.

But that thought made Sarah feel more sober than ever. Just to think! In two weeks Kathleen would become Mrs. Herbie Gerrick. And then she'd be gone. Even if she came back from far-off California after two years or so, she'd never come home and be just plain Kathleen Scott anymore.

"I think weddings are terribly exciting. Don't you?" said Linda. When Sarah didn't answer her, Linda looked around in surprise. "Why—why—Sarah! Oh, I'm sorry!"

But Sarah darted from the room. *I'm not going to cry,* she thought fiercely. *I'm not going to!* "Got to s-start s-supper," she called back.

Lots of leftovers were stored in the pantry. A whole big roasterful of chicken—wings and backs and necks, all the bony pieces. They're pretty good eating, if you weren't in too great a rush. And there were bowlfuls of creamed vegetables and things too. Mashed potatoes— gravy. About seven kinds of pie all jumbled together in one cake tin. Sarah could get the fires going, and shove the roaster into the oven. Just shaking down the damper of the stove, and laying the kindling, and nursing the fire till it was snapping helped her forget the lump in her throat.

Supper turned out to be pretty cheerful after all. Robbie wanted to know about school.

"Miss Haliday handed out the readers," chattered Sarah between nibbles at a chicken wing.

"And I guess you've read yours through by now," he said.

"No, I haven't!" she said. "We-ell, I sort of skimmed through it—"

"Ho! I can imagine!"

Well, he needn't tease. He liked reading just as much as she did.

"The stories look terribly interesting, some of 'em. And guess what! We got a whole boxful of new books for the library. Kathleen, did you ever read *Lorna Doone?* That's one of 'em. And *Westward Ho!* and *Children of the New Forest* and—oh, yes—there's a brand new *Anne of Green Gables!*"

"Is there?" said Kathleen. "The old copy must have been new about the time I was your age."

Ten years ago! Sarah Naomi was only a few months old then.

That started a do-you-remember-when sort of talk. Robbie told about the time he found Sarah in the pantry—she could barely walk!—with two whole pounds of butter smeared all over her stockings and new brown boots. Felt boots, with leather tips.

Kathleen groaned, laughing. "The shoes were ruined, of course. And once I found her up to her elbows in jam."

Linda laughed till her cheeks ached. She wanted to hear more and more about Sarah's pranks when she was a baby.

"What a mischief!" she exclaimed. "What else did she do? Tell, Kathleen. You don't mind, do you, Sarah?"

Sarah shook her head, smiling. People didn't remember things like that about you unless they thought you were pretty special.

This evening, after supper, they had a once-a-year chore to do that was always fun. Sarah had seen the newly washed bedticking hanging on the line. This was tick-filling day on the Scott farm.

"We'll do it first thing, before dark," said Kathleen. "The dishes can wait."

Robbie took the ticks off the line and went racing down the hill to the straw pile. Linda begged to watch the fun, so Kathleen took her downhill in the wheelbarrow. Brindle's calf had taken a liking to Linda, so he pranced alongside. And Daisy's and Beauty's spring colts, big leggy things now, came trotting to investigate. Spencer romped all over and around everybody. So they had a lot of company.

Tumbling about in the fresh-smelling straw was part of the fun each year. Then grabbing fistfuls of it, and thrusting your arm up to the shoulder into the ticks. The cases grew fat and stiff. They had to be trundled separately up hill at last, squeezed through the garden gate, through the door—and dragged and pushed up the stairs and onto the beds.

It was fun to make the bed with a new straw mattress on it.

"And just think," said Kathleen. "This winter you'll have your rustling nest entirely to yourself."

"*Don't*, Kathleen," Sarah protested.

"Why, chickie! Why, Sarah Naomi!" The last words came out very softly.

They were alone. Sarah stood at the window, with her forehead resting on the center ledge. She hadn't meant to cry. She wasn't going to. But, big tears began plopping onto the windowsill.

Kathleen slipped her arm around Sarah. And a few of the drops that fell now didn't come from Sarah at all. Then Kathleen blew her nose.

"Aren't you happy for me?" she said.

Sarah nodded ever so slightly.

"Well, what's wrong then? Don't you like Herbie?"

"You *know* I do!" said Sarah hotly.

Kathleen laughed a shaky laugh. "That's more like my spunky sister. Look, I won't love you any less when I'm Kathleen Gerrick than I do now. I *promise*. And you'll have a big brother again. Think of that! Herbie thinks you're pretty wonderful, do you know that?"

So they cheered up together.

"Well, anyway," said Sarah with a decided nod of her head, "anyway I've still got Linda. Aunt Jane told Mother that Linda would most likely be staying here with us for a long, long time."

"And I'm so happy to hear she has received Jesus as her Saviour. She says it happened in the meadow yesterday—and that you helped her."

"Yes. But mostly it was Susan," Sarah said.

She went *ka-thump-ka-thump* down the stairs quite happily, setting down first her toes and then her heel at each step. Kathleen had gone skimming down ahead of her.

Linda— They would be together, and every day they would keep on praying and exercising. And one day—who knew?—Linda might be walking again! God could heal her.

The telephone shrilled—two longs, two shorts. Just as Sarah ka-thumped down the last steps she heard Kathleen say, "Hello?"

It must be long distance calling! Maybe from as far away as Saskatoon! Kathleen's voice went higher.

"Yes—yes—Kathleen Scott speaking—" she said. "What was that? Would you mind repeating?— Central, could you catch that?— Linda Bolton? Yes—yes—Miss Jane Bolton's still in the hospital. Yes, she's improving, but— Yes, I can hear you more clearly now— Yes— Oh, I see! I see—I—I see! Yes, Mr. Bolton—"

Mister Bolton!

Kathleen turned from the telephone, and her cheeks were scarlet with excitement. "Linda, darling, guess who this is."

"My daddy!" said Linda.

"Telephoning from Ottawa," said Kathleen. "He'd like to talk to you."

Kathleen and Robbie propped her up so she could talk into the mouthpiece. She was almost too excited to bring out a sound though—too excited and too happy. Her father had news for her. He would be stationed in Ottawa now. As soon as Aunt Jane was able to travel she and Linda were to join him there. They would have a home together and they'd be near the best doctors!

Linda was shaking when they lowered her to the couch again. Her eyes were like blue stars. "Oh, Sarah Naomi, I'll see Daddy again! Just think!"

"We're very happy for you, Linda. All of us," said Kathleen gently. "Now you'd better go to bed. You've had quite a day."

Later, Robbie went outdoors and fed the calves and closed the chicken house while Kathleen and Sarah did the dishes.

"I guess," said Sarah as she slid another warm plate onto the stack of newly wiped ones, "I guess if it was *me*—and if I hadn't seen Father in ever so long—"

"Exactly," said Kathleen.

Sarah lay awake for a long, long time that night though. For one thing, she felt strange perched high on the new mattress. The stalks of straw seemed to whisper secrets to each other. If they really could, what stories would they tell? About the summer winds and rains, maybe? Or the nests of the field mice—

Because the mattress was so fat, it was narrower too, so Sarah had to take care not to roll off. During the night a hollow formed where she had slept—a nest, Kathleen had called it.

Sarah's big sister sat at the table near the flowery lamp, stitching at her wedding petticoat. It had a lacy top. Kathleen thought Sarah was asleep. When the front door downstairs opened and closed, Kathleen picked up the lamp and tiptoed out of the room with it.

Mother must be home—but Sarah felt too drowsy to get out of bed now. Kathleen would tell the news. But maybe Mother knew already. The Slocums were on the same party line—and Mrs. Slocum always listened to other people's calls. She thought that was part of being a helpful neighbor. You never knew. They might be in trouble.

Maybe she'd been too busy today though, with the threshing crew to feed and all—

The next thing, Sarah found herself beside the Thatcher machine. How had she gotten here? Straw was coming out of the blower, sifting down and sifting down. She tried to run away but her feet were glued to the ground. It was all right though. The straw was coming down as soft and gentle as snowflakes. It kept piling up around her. But suddenly she wasn't afraid at all.

Sarah slept.

When she awoke it was to hear the soft hiss of rain on the roof. It was trickling along the eaves troughs too. If there was enough rain to drip from the eaves, it was enough to stop the threshing for the day—that's what Father always said. Poor Mrs. Slocum! With all that good food ready and no crew to eat it.

But the rain also meant that Father and Stuart would stay at home today. Suddenly, Sarah remembered Linda's telephone call. She hurried to get dressed so she could hear the family discussion. If it rained hard enough, she might get to stay at home with Linda, and they could begin making the bride doll!

Mother stood looking out the kitchen window when Sarah came skimming down the stairs. "What do you think, Father? Should the children go to school?" Mother said.

Sarah could guess what his answer would be. For almost three weeks he and Stuart had been up early and late, early and late. He would think there was nothing better to do on a rainy day than to have a good long nap. Two 10-year-old girls in the house chattering and giggling might disturb his sleep.

What he said was, "It's not a cold rain. And we have waterproof blankets. What do *you* think, Mother?"

"If you say so," said Mother.

And that's the way the matter was decided.

Sarah didn't really mind. And neither did Robbie. If rain kept falling there'd be few pupils in school. Then Miss Haliday would let them do just about as they pleased, provided they were quiet. With new books in the library, both Robbie and Sarah would be well and happily occupied.

It rained most of the day, but when Wally went splashing home through the puddles that afternoon, the gray clouds looked like one vast circular tent, with all the side curtains rolled up. Sarah could see a sunny blue sky all around. So when she walked into the living room the sun was striking the windows. At first she thought that was what made Linda's face glow.

"Oh, Sarah, Sarah!" squealed Linda, hugging herself because Sarah wasn't close enough. "Guess what! Your dad spoke to my dad today. And it's all arranged. As soon as threshing is done—and the wedding over, and the potatoes are dug and all—guess what! Oh, you'd never guess!"

"Your father is coming for you," said Sarah promptly.

"Wrong. But it's almost as nice. Your dad and mom are going to travel to Ottawa with me and Aunt Jane. What do you think of *that?* Dad is going to pay for their trip. Honest, I was dreadfully afraid to go with strangers. Having Aunt Sheila there—why, it'll be lovely."

She was so happy and so relieved. Sarah didn't want to spoil her joy. But she carried a very sober face into the kitchen.

"It will be for one month only," comforted Mother, speaking low. "We hoped to tell you ourselves, Father and I, but never mind."

A month. A whole month!

"It would seem a shame not to do some visiting while we are there, wouldn't it? Both Father and I have relatives in the East, and we haven't seen any of them in years."

Kathleen—Linda—Mother—Father— One by one and two by two they were going!

Sarah thought of the verses Father read in devotions one morning lately. About a little sparrow all alone on a housetop—and about a pelican in a watery wilderness—

Once, on a First of July outing, Father rowed Sarah clear across Loon Lake, through the narrows, and onto Pelican Lake. There was an island in the middle. The pelican colony perched there, about 15 of them that day. Each bird sat hunched and lonesome-looking, staring into space.

Well, that was exactly how Sarah felt today.

CHAPTER 5

A Very Special Wedding

IF YOU DIDN'T LET yourself think too much of the sad part, a wedding in the family was an exciting thing. It was a pretty important event.

At school all the big girls were friendly as anything with Sarah now. At recess and during the noon hour each day, they would crowd around her. They admired her hair (it was the same old hair, blackish and reddish) and they admired her complexion (but she still had 11 freckles on her nose). They coaxed her to tell if she was going to be bridesmaid and what kind of dress Kathleen was going to wear and about the wedding luncheon and everything.

Usually, everybody at Braeburn ate *dinner* at noon and *supper* in the evening. They were everydayish names. *Luncheon* was an elegant word.

At home things went pretty much the same way. Father had been getting a bit restless—and Stuart more than a bit—because of the wet spell of weather. Stuart said several times a day that it really was *high time* he began his grade 12 studies in Blakely high school. He'd lag so far behind his classmates, he'd never be able to catch up. Both Father and Stuart thought they ought to dig the potatoes now, while they were waiting for the grain to dry after the rains. But Mother shook her head.

"I'm afraid I'm too busy. Besides, we'd absolutely ruin our hands. Unless you menfolks want to do the job alone—"

But that wasn't the Scott way. This was a family job. Father always ploughed up the potatoes with a hand plow while the rest of them went stoop-stooping behind him, picking up the big and little potatoes. Then Father stored them in the cellar for winter. If everybody helped it was a one-day job.

"Well, what do you say, boys?" said Father. "With the princess to help—"

Sarah opened her mouth, but Mother spoke up first. "Sorry, John. Sarah can't. She *is* the bride's sister."

"Oh, look at her strut!" hooted Robbie. "Think you're pretty important, don't you, Miss Sarah Naomi Scott!"

"I thought Kathleen was planning a simple wedding," said Father, tweaking Sarah's nearest pigtail.

"And so she is," said Mother. "But Sarah is to be in charge of the guest book."

That's the way things went these days. The potato digging had to wait. The wedding was more important.

The luncheon would be served in a tent—a marquee, Kathleen called it. There'd be long tables under the marquee, just about where the 40 threshers had eaten. Hoooo, 40! This time they would have about 200 people in the yard, visiting around, eating dainty sandwiches and salads, and fancy cookies and cakes.

Each day now, from early morning to late at night, the oven was busy. Mother did the baking, Kathleen did the icing and decorating. Kathleen's was the pretty job. Sometimes Linda got to help her. But Sarah? Each day when she rushed home from school, she found another stack of pans and mixing bowls and spoons to wash.

One wedding job of hers was more interesting, really funny too. Just about every day Father came home with an armload of parcels for the bride. Wedding presents! Kathleen got to open them, but Sarah made a list of who sent what.

"*Another* set of water glasses," Sarah said. "Who's it from?"

Mother had a funny look on her face. Kathleen and Herbie had 70 water glasses now, but not a single knife or fork. When he heard, Father laughed till his shoulders shook. But Herbie and Kathleen didn't seem to mind anything.

Herbie came every day to help prepare. On the day before the wedding, he helped raise the tent and put up tables. Once though when Sarah had gone to her secret hiding place under the crab apple tree, for a private thinking time, she saw Kathleen and Herbie standing in the garden path. Just *standing* there, looking at each other. Their faces gave Sarah a funny tingly feeling.

That was the way Father and Mother sometimes looked at each other.

It might happen when Father glanced up from reading aloud to her on Sunday evening—or when he came home late from the field, all dusty and tired, and Mother brought him a basinful of warm water and some clean, soft, nice-smelling cloths to use for towels—or when he carried a cup of tea to her when she had been working especially hard.

You're wonderful. Why, I guess you're the most wonderful person in all the whole wide world! was what the look seemed to say. A private sort of thing.

Sarah snuggled lower in her hiding place. She took a handful of little apples from her bulging pocket and crunched the crabs slowly until the path was empty again.

Just when she crawled out, she heard the high, far-off cries of a flock of Canada geese. And there they were—a big wavering V against the blue sky. *Good-bye, good-bye,* they seemed to be calling. *Summer's over. We're flying south—*

Sarah's eyes pricked, and she had a lump in her throat.

Some things are *right,* even if they make you feel sad. Like the geese going south, and Kathleen leaving home. They are right because God planned them that way.

"Wherever have you been?" said Mother when Sarah slipped into the kitchen a few minutes later. "Didn't you remember—we still have your dress to fit!"

It was made of shot shantung! If you looked at it one way it was green—another way and it was yellow. A wide rustling belt of traffeta went with it. And she had a matching ribbon on her straw hat. Mother painted the hat with green paint, so it was stiff and shiny as new too. It squeaked. And the roll brim was pinned back by a cluster of yellow roses. Sarah even had a pair of patent sandals! She had begged for *real* artificial silk stockings. Susan Gerrick was going to wear some. But Mother decided that fine cotton would be more practical for Sarah.

Tomorrow, thought Sarah. *Tomorrow—*

Her hair was all done up in rags tonight, so it would hang in curls tomorrow. After all, she was the bride's *sister*. But the lumpy rags kept her awake for a while.

Tomorrow began with a sneeze!

Sarah opened her eyes. Kathleen was stooping over her, laughing silently. She had tickled Sarah's lip with a feather.

"Hey, sleepyhead!" she whispered. "Want to come with me?"

Sarah sat up, wide awake instantly. "Where to?"

"Shh! To round up the cows!"

That was no chore for a bride on her wedding day!

"Just us two?" said Sarah.

"Just we two. But be quiet as a mouse."

Sarah giggled and hurried into her clothes. They tiptoed down the stairs in their stockings, stopping whenever a board creaked. It was early—about 5:30. In the kitchen they put on their shoes. Kathleen draped Stuart's jacket around Sarah's shoulders and slipped into Father's. They laughed silently at the droopy shoulders and sleeves.

Outdoors, the morning was sunny and cool. All the grass was dripping with dew. Spencer crawled out of his house, and shook himself and yawned. He didn't like the wet, but he came trotting at their heels just the same.

The yard looked strange because of the big tent that covered so much of it. But the meadow was just like always. Kathleen and Sarah talked aloud now, following the wiggly cow path. They picked flowers—Queen Anne's lace and asters and wild sunflowers. Every little while Kathleen would stop to look—up at the trees and around at the hills and the creek. She had a listening look on her face. A meadowlark was singing and singing.

She and Sarah laughed a lot. But for a few minutes, they talked about serious things too—about serving Jesus, and never turning back. About praying for each other, always and always—

Perhaps the cows were a bit surprised to be rounded up so early. (But Spencer did most of the work.) They came without a fuss.

"Look at your *feet!*" exclaimed Mother when they returned to the house. Their shoes and stockings were drenched. "Kathleen, whatever were you *thinking* of? What if both of you should come down with a cold today, of all days!"

"We won't, will we, Kathleen?" said Sarah.

"I hope not," Kathleen said. "The morning was so lovely, I couldn't resist, Mother." Then she added something about "one last time." But Sarah scampered upstairs as fast as she could because she didn't want to be reminded.

Last night was Thursday night, not Saturday at all. But the Scotts gathered around the organ after supper to sing and play. *One last time.* Nobody said the words, but everyone must have been thinking them. And that was just as bad.

Herbie was there too, standing behind Kathleen as she played. They sang all the family favorites. Then Father asked for "Will the Circle Be Unbroken?" It was a mistake. He was the very first to stop singing. One by one all the others stopped too, till only the organ kept on.

Somehow though, this morning, Sarah felt better after her walk with Kathleen. She rubbed her feet and put on dry things and raced downstairs.

After that it was hurry, hurry, hurry. Eat breakfast. Pick

flowers for the tables. Get dressed in your wedding things. Watch Father and Kathleen leave for church.

The rest of the family was going in Aunt Jane's sedan, with Stuart driving! Aunt Jane sent a message saying she'd be absolutely *cross* if they didn't use her car. But Father and Kathleen were going in the top buggy with Hyacinthe. They wanted it that way. Sarah couldn't see why.

Father looked very trim and proud as anything when he helped Kathleen into the buggy—with her armful of roses and her veil and all. Hyacinthe pawed the ground. She was a pretty smart trotter, but all the same the buggy had to leave home about a half hour before the others.

Mother peeked into the pantry to make sure everything was ready for the reception. She worried about having enough kindling to get a fire going quickly when the people would begin coming. Last of all she combed Sarah's curls, brushing and brushing them. Sarah could hardly stand still. Everything took so *long* today.

But finally they all got into the car. Mother sat beside Stuart. Linda, Sarah, and Robbie sat in the back seat. Imagine breezing along like this! It was a bit hot though. All the glass windows were closed, so the wind couldn't muss their curls and ribbons and things.

Long before they could see the gables of the church, they passed Hyacinthe. Stuart pressed the croaking horn, and Hyacinthe began galloping!

"Stuart!" said Mother.

But Sarah, twisting her head around, could see Father's strong hands on the reins. Both he and Kathleen were laughing. She waved before the car scuttled up the hill and the buggy dropped out of sight.

The churchyard was simply crammed with cars and buggies. Quite a few of the guests never came to church on Sundays at all. Suddenly, Sarah had a funny feeling—as if all of this was a dream. Herbie's brother Ralph was one usher, Stuart the other. And that seemed unreal. They stuck out their elbows and Susan and Sarah were supposed to slip their hands into the crooks—just like ladies!—and walk down the aisle with their brothers. Past Linda, who sat in an armchair under the balcony—past a lot of ladies in fancy hats—right up to the second pew, so they'd be real close to the bride and groom.

Robbie came to sit beside Sarah. Chuck and Bertie Gerrick squeezed past Susan. All three boys looked scrubbed and unfamiliar with their hair slicked into place for once. Just as the ushers brought their mothers in, Sister Hammond began playing the organ. This must be real. The organ sounded real enough. It gasped and squeaked just the way it did on Sundays.

Next, the door near the platform swung open. Out came Brother Hammond and Herbie. Hey, where was Kathleen?

"Sit still!" said Robbie, barely whispering it. "They're coming."

And they were. The music changed. It was soft and sweet now. The gasps could hardly be heard. And there came Kathleen and Father. Kathleen was all shimmery. White, with goldy lace down the front, and the veil and roses and all—she looked dreamy too. Father's face was serious and sort of pale under the tan. But Kathleen was smiling—at Herbie!

First thing Brother Hammond did was to ask a surprising question. "Who giveth this woman in marriage?"

Didn't he *know?*

Well, Father settled that in a hurry. "I do," he said in his deep Sunday School superintendent voice.

So then Herbie knew it was all right, and he came to get Kathleen, and Father sat down beside Sarah. It was like play acting.

But—it wasn't, really.

"Do you, Herbert William Gerrick, take this woman to be your wedded wife. . . ?" There were a lot more words, but that was all Sarah really heard. She couldn't help wondering why they always called Kathleen "this woman." It didn't sound polite.

The next minute Herbie was "this man!"

"Do you, Kathleen Mary Scott, take this man to be your wedded husband. . . ?"

Robbie nudged Sarah's elbow. His eyes were laughing. He jerked his chin toward the platform. Then Sarah saw— A mouse had come to the wedding! She poked her head out from behind the organ several times. Then she must have decided it was safe to come out all the way. She ran across the platform, down the steps, just sort of gliding down—and she headed straight for Mrs. Gerrick!

"Eek!" said Herbie's mother softly, and stuck her feet straight before her.

"Eek!" said the lady behind her just as softly, and up came her feet.

By now there was a rustle in church. Some people were coughing. Chuckie Gerrick had his eyes closed and his mouth locked, and he was rocking from side to side, his face as red as a rooster's comb. Robbie snorted once and then he coughed into his hanky. Even Father's shoulder shivered for a moment.

Sarah couldn't tell if Herbie and Kathleen had noticed their little guest at all. Brother Hammond asked them to kneel, and the whole church became hushed. He prayed for them. Then they prayed. They asked God to lead them so they would always live for Him. Father was wiping his eyes now, and Sarah slipped her hand into his other one. The next thing she knew Herbie and Kathleen were facing all the people, smiling happily.

"It gives me pleasure," said Brother Hammond, and he was smiling too, "it gives me *great* pleasure to present Mr. and Mrs. Herbert Gerrick!"

There was no Kathleen Scott anymore.

After that came the ride home. It was a race to get there before any of the other cars arrived. Then came the people, people trampling through the garden, sitting or standing around in all the rooms in the house, sitting at the long tables under the marquee. Long processions of women and girls moved in and out of the kitchen carrying platters and plates filled with fancy salads and sandwiches and cakes. Susan and Sarah got to help serve.

Their sandals were soundless on the grass. They flitted here and there, hearing bits of talk. The bits got jumbled, and it was funny.

"Disgraceful!" (That was Susan's ma.) "A mouse in church! The janitor ought to. . ."

"Salt it down overnight. Then in the morning you add three cups of vinegar. . . ."

". . . and yards of gold lace! Charming combination. Charming bride!"

"But," said old Mr. Cavendish, sounding fierce. He had heard the last remark too. "But she don't come within a mile of the way Sheila Murray looked at *her* wedding."

Sheila Murray was *Mother!*

About six men were in a huddle at the south end of the long table. They thought Herbie and Kathleen's wedding was pretty tame. Nothing to drink. (But most of them had cupfuls of tea or coffee!) And no dancing— Not like Jack and Sheila Scott's wedding had been.

They said something else, something about Keith. Sarah wasn't sure she had understood though. And just that moment someone coughed, and someone muttered that saying about little pitchers having big ears. It's what grown-ups say to other grown-ups. It's a sort of signal that warns, *Watch out. Child nearby. Might understand.* And all the time they think you don't know they are talking about you!

After that it was Sarah's turn to eat. Braeburn school got out early today, so a lot of the boys and girls were eating at the same table. It was noisy, but fun too. Then Miss Haliday came to shoo them out into the yard for a game of drop the hanky. But they had barely started when someone yelled that the bride and groom were going now. Everyone raced to see them off.

The runabout stood in front of the garden gate. The rumble seat was jammed with suitcases and boxes, and Herbie had tied a canvas sheet over the things. Kathleen was wearing her new navy and white outfit. There were kisses and hugs, and a lot of talking and laughing.

Then they drove away. Sarah stood watching, and she felt proud of herself. She hadn't cried—not a single tear.

CHAPTER 6

Aunt Jane's Auction Sale

SARAH SEEMED to be walking through a huge, tumble-down castle. Oh, immense! For a long, long time she had been stumbling through interesting but scary rooms and along dark passages. Now she had come to the hall of echoes. Someone told her that that was its name. Someone was demonstrating, by calling her name.

"Sarah-ah-ah-ah-ah-ah. . . .

"Sarah-ah-ah-ah-ah-ah. . . ."

Funny. The voice sounded hollow, the way it does when you shout into a rain barrel. She wondered if it would sound like that if *she* said the name. But she couldn't. She tried. Only a squeak came out. Then—

"Sarah Naomi Scott!"

She jerked—and opened her eyes. The castle was gone! She was in her own bed, in her own room. (It was her very own now that Kathleen was gone.) She blinked sleepily. The closet was half-empty, with all of Kathleen's things missing. But the flowery lamp sat on the table. Kathleen had left it for her. In the city she would have electricity!

"Sarah!" It was her mother calling.

She sat up in her rustling bed. "Yes—Mother," she answered sleepily.

"Time to get up," her mother said. "Today is potato-digging day. Are you sure you're awake?"

"Yes, Mother." She said more briskly this time.

She slid out of bed and stretched and yawned.

Yesterday she and Kathleen had crept down the stairs and had the lovely walk. That was the way the wedding day had begun. It ended when most of the Braeburn pupils were playing ball in the meadow near the creek. They saw the tent flutter and swoop, flutter and swoop, clear to the ground. Then one by one the poles teetered and fell. By the time they came up the hill, all of the tent parts were packed in their special wagon box. Mr. Heathe was taking it to Paxton this morning. Some ladies had helped Mother wash the floors and put all the furniture back where it belonged. The big day was over.

Sarah called down the stairs now. "Mother? What shall I wear?"

"Put on your oldest dress," Mother said. "The green plaid gingham."

That patched thing! For months it had hung on a nail. Sarah giggled when she looked at it. The nail had left such a pucker that there would be room for a big boil between her shoulder blades. The dress was awfully short too.

She slipped into it and sat down on the topmost step with her legs stretched out. She let herself slide, bumpety-bump, to the bottom of the flight.

"Well, there you are!" exclaimed Mother, who was busily

stirring porridge. "Quickly get washed and set the table. You'll have to remember now: you're our biggest girl at home."

Sarah rolled her eyes and leaned her tousled head against Mother's arm for a moment.

"I'm the littlest too, remember?" she murmured.

Mother tried to look stern, but a tiny smile escaped. "So you are, Sarah. But you and I will have to divide Kathleen's work between us, I'm afraid." Then she sighed. "I feel sometimes that my children have had to grow up too fast."

"Oh, we don't mind," said Sarah comfortingly. "We like work." And for the moment she really felt that way.

The first thing after breakfast, Stuart and Robbie picked up the wagon tongue and started pulling the wagon toward the potato patch. Sarah pushed for a bit. But then the boys began prancing and trotting like a pair of frisky horses. She took a firm grip, lifted her feet off the ground, drew up her knees, and hung on, swinging and bobbing. Tall pigweed whipped her cheek. She hung on. The upside-down ride lasted clear to the edge of the potato patch behind the poplar grove. There she dropped to her feet again, laughing.

Father had gone to the machine shed. In the farthest musty dusty corner stood the hand plow that Grandfather Scott brought to Canada with him more than 100 years ago. Wally came at a sober trot now, pulling the plow. At the north end of the rows, Father dug in the plowshare. He clucked to Wally—and behind them the earth began turning. All the big and little and middle-sized potatoes came into view.

Mother and Sarah, Stuart and Robbie, all trailed the plow. Potato picking isn't easy. But it could be a sort of special day. There were the sun and the wind, and the smell of moist earth. And hundreds of firm potatoes clunking into the pails. And pailfuls of potatoes tumbling into gunnysacks. And sackfuls of potatoes hoisted over the side of the high wagon box. And at last, the lantern light falling on big bins in the cellar, all filled to the brim with satin-skinned potatoes!

A rich, earthy smell was all around then. And you had a thanksgiving feeling in your heart.

But everyone was stiff as could be that Saturday night. It was pretty late. All the chores had to be done at Aunt Jane's and the Scotts'. And bathtime was still ahead. Dinner had been nothing except wedding leftovers, eaten cold. So Mother was cooking a rich beef stew and baking potatoes to go with it.

Sarah set the table. When that was done she went to be with Linda for a bit. All this long day Linda had been working on her Kathleen bride doll. Sarah sank to her knees beside the couch and rested her cheek on a pillow while she listened to Linda.

"I got the dress just about finished. See, this lace goes here, and. . . ."

Something odd was happening to Linda's voice. It grew fuzzier and fuzzier, and it came in waves. Pretty soon that was all that was left—*bzz*—like the bumbling of a bumble-bee.

Sarah was falling asleep right there on her knees.

She was wide awake when supper was ready though. This Saturday night there was no singing at the Scott home. Partly because it was so late. Partly—though no-body mentioned this—because they would miss Kathleen too much. Mother played one hymn softly on the organ. Then Father led devotions. Sarah got first chance at the tub. She fell asleep as soon as she snuggled down in the straw nest and pulled the patchwork quilt up to her chin.

The following Monday was the day that Stuart went back to high school. Hyacinthe pawed and snorted, excited as anything. Stuart tried not to show it, but he was just as excited. All of them watched him drive off. Except Father, of course. He left home at four this morning. The grain was dry enough to thresh now. About four more days of threshing were left for the Thatcher machine.

After that Monday, the days passed like beads slipping from a string. There was no knot at the end and you couldn't stop them. Pretty soon there would be none left. Pretty soon the last morning would come, and Father, Mother, and Linda would leave for the East.

It was a sad thought. But in a way it gave Sarah a proud feeling too. She and Robbie and Stuart would be keeping house alone!

Every evening now Sarah milked Bessie, the Ayrshire. She got to milk Bessie, because she was the gentlest cow and the easiest to milk. Sarah could milk her outdoors or indoors, it didn't matter. Bessie stood perfectly still, unless the flies were bad outdoors. And even *then* she might walk away, but she never kicked.

Sarah liked outdoors best. For three days the redwing blackbirds held a convention in the poplar grove! It was fun to hear all the whistling. Sometimes the hundreds of birds chirped away at the same time. Robbie said they were singing, "O Canada!" Then one bird would hop to the topmost branch and give a long talk. He might be interrupted though, and someone else take his place.

Sarah leaned her head against Bessie's silky flank. Pull—squeeze—pull—squeeze— That was what milking was all about. You had to squeeze with a sort of rolling motion. Your arms got tired and trembly. But the jets of milk frothed down into the pail. Ginger and Spencer usually lay nearby. Sometimes Ginger rose to pat Sarah's knee with one paw. This was a ladylike hint. *I like warm milk. Remember?* So Sarah would send a squirt her way, right into her open mouth. It went hissing in, hardly a drop spilling.

This year Sarah had another autumn chore. Mother had scrubbed all the storm windows. All summer long they were stored on the rafters in the machine shed. They were dusty and cobwebby as anything when Stuart and Robbie carried them to the house.

Because of the sunny weather Mother scrubbed them outdoors on the grass. Then she spread a white paste all over the glass. This dried in about a minute. Then it was Sarah's job to wipe off the paste and polish the glass on both sides. Forty-eight panes in all!

Threshing was over. For a few days afterwards, Father hauled oat sheaves from the field and stacked them behind the barn. Stuart and Robbie helped him in the evenings and on Saturday. But Father's main job now was to get ready for the auction sale over at Aunt Jane's place.

She was getting better, a little better each day the doctor said. But she didn't expect to live on her farm again. At first she thought she'd sell only the live things—chickens, pigs, and cattle. But now she had decided to sell the furniture, the farm implements, *everything*.

An auction sale can be terribly exciting. This would be a big one. Bills were posted on telephone poles every few miles. Hundreds of people would come.

After school on the day before the sale Sarah hurried home. Robbie had missed school today to help. When Sarah reached Aunt Jane's place, she headed Wally up the lane instead of going on. Linda was there! She sat in an armchair in the shade of the lilac bush. That was one surprise. But the whole yard looked strange. The implements were lined up near the barn. The household things were arranged in a sort of circle near the garden gate—all the things of which Aunt Jane had taken such good care. Dressers, bedsteads, bedsprings, tables, chairs, chesterfield. Today there were a lonesome and sad-looking jumble.

Sarah went to peek into all the empty rooms. The house echoed, almost like that castle in her dreams. The walls were bare. The windows looked naked with no curtains and shades there. The dining room was jammed though. All the mattresses were leaning against the walls with heaps of rugs and things filling up the middle. These were the things that would be spoiled if they got wet from rain or dew.

And in the kitchen Mother and Mrs. Heathe were cutting ring bologna—oh, 100 pounds or more of it!—into three-inch pieces. Tomorrow everybody who came to the sale would get free lunch—a paper bag with two pieces of sausage, two buns, and an apple.

This evening at the supper table Sarah begged hard to be allowed to miss school.

"Susan and her brothers aren't going to be in school," she said. "Some of the others aren't either. Stella Thatcher, Johnny Siddons, and oh, a lot of others."

"Well, what do you say, Mother?" said Father.

"If *you* say so," said Mother.

It was their way of saying, *I don't object if you don't.* It was as good as a yes.

"Whee!" said Sarah, clasping her hands so hard she squashed her buttered bun flat as a gingersnap.

But later Sarah thought of something—the problem of Linda. The crowds and crowds of people over at Aunt Jane's would tire her dreadfully. She'd have no place to rest. Besides, it might be sad for her to see Aunt Jane's things being sold. Take today. She was very quiet, sitting under the lilac bush. And she had hardly said a word. So?

Sarah was drying dishes. "Do you think I'd better stay home—with Linda?" She spoke in a whisper. The living room door was open.

Mother answered in a low voice. "Do you really want to?"

Sarah gulped. "I want to—and I *don't* want to. I guess Linda shouldn't have to be there though."

"No, she shouldn't. But if you were in school she'd have to go. I'm needed over there. Still, if you want to make this sacrifice, I know the Lord will be pleased."

"I guess we'd better do it that way," said Sarah, and she sighed a bit.

However, before Sarah got to telling Linda, a telephone call changed her plans again. It was Mrs. Gerrick. She said Susan offered to stay with Linda. She didn't really like auction sales much. Not like sales!

From an upstairs window next morning, Sarah could see the people beginning to arrive. Father left early, walking across the field. Robbie was driving Mother and Sarah over in the two-seater buggy. He could hardly wait to get going. Aunt Jane's car stood in line with the implements today. It was going to be sold along with the other things. Stuart and Hyacinthe left for Blakely just the same as other days. An auction sale wasn't important enough to stop Stuart.

Sarah danced down the stairs in her newest blue-checked dress this morning. Kathleen sewed it the week before the wedding. Mother made Sarah take a sweater too, in case the day should turn cold. They waited only long enough for Susan to come. Then Robbie clucked to Prince and Captain, and they were off. All the same, Aunt Jane's yard was pretty crowded by the time they got there. The auctioneer, a big man—big up and down and big all around—was just about to begin.

He stood on a wagon. Mr. Darnley handed things up to him. Father sat at a table nearby, writing down everything that was sold and for how much and to whom.

Mothers sat in Aunt Jane's best chairs, visiting in the sun. Their babies rolled in the grass at their feet. Older children climbed over things, peeked into things, ducked under grown-ups' elbows, or wiggled between their feet. Noise and fuss, excitement and laughter filled the air. The auctioneer teased the people, and they teased him right back. He told make-believe stories about some of Aunt Jane's things, just to be funny.

At noon most of the boys and girls took their bags of sausage, bun, and apple and climbed into the big haymow. After eating they tumbled on the hay awhile. They imitated the auctioneer's jumble of words. Johnny Siddons said that what Mr. Waite said was "Rubble - dubble - snubble - rattle - tattle - pattle - yellow - bellow - dellow - corble - morble - torkle - freckle - leckle - heckle - finkle - dinkle - wrinkle——and SOLD!"

So everybody practiced saying it, chanting the sounds faster and faster, and laughing like anything.

From the little side door up there, Sarah watched as Aunt Jane's horses and cows were led into the ring one by one to be sold. Finally nothing was left but a few pieces that nobody wanted. The sale was over.

And now all the autumn chores were done. Now there was nothing to keep Father and Mother at home any longer.

So the last morning came. For a going-away present, Linda gave Sarah the Kathleen bride doll. They promised to write to each other often and never to forget each other and to pray for each other.

"You must tell me the minute your legs get better," said Sarah.

Linda looked wistful and excited. "You really believe they're going to be well again?"

Sarah nodded. "God can. And you and Susan and me are praying the where-two-or-three-agree prayer. And Mother and Father are praying too, and I guess so are Kathleen and Herbie, and Stuart and Robbie— So!"

It was harder—and easier—to say good-bye to Father and Mother. They were going to be back in a month. But they had never been gone so long before.

Father had a lot of do's and don'ts for them to remember. Coral, the purebred Jersey heifer, had never had a calf before. Sometimes young cows could be really fierce when their babies arrived. Father expected to be back in time, but if not, and if there was trouble, Robbie or Stuart should be sure to call Mr. Slocum. He knew just about all there was to know about cows and horses. He had promised to keep an eye on the stock here.

Mother's do's and don'ts had to do with fires and wearing rubbers when it rained and eating regular meals and not staying up too late to read.

They were leaving from Paxton on the evening train. Mr. Slocum was taking them all in the car, so Robbie and

Sarah got to ride along. They watched the steam locomotive pound past the station. They even paid Aunt Jane a brief visit where she rested in her berth. They inspected the berths where Linda and Mother would be sleeping. And they waved from the platform when the train pulled out again. The bell clanged, the train whistled, and then it whisked away down the track. The last Sarah saw was a puff of steam and smoke with a black blur under it. Then the train was out of sight.

CHAPTER 7

A Taste of Independence

ON THE WAY HOME Sarah sat between Mr. Slocum and Robbie. The lights were dimming and brightening, dimming and brightening. So Mr. Slocum was going no more than 20 miles per hour. She heard him tell Robbie so.

For a wonder Mr. Slocum spoke quietly. He must think she was asleep. Her eyes were closed a lot of the time, but she was thinking.

Mostly of Father, and of a talk they had after Aunt Jane's sale.

Mother and Robbie hurried home to do the chores that evening. Father had to stay to the end, so Sarah asked to stay too. After the last people had gone they padlocked all the buildings. Then they walked home together, cutting across the field. It was only a bit more than a half mile that way. The sun was down but the moon was shining. Everything looks different by moonlight, sort of magicked. Cows and horses can look huge, oh, *enormous!* It's a bit scary when you're alone. But Father was there.

At first there was the crisp stubble under her shoes, but

then they climbed through the fence, and came to the meadow. That was silent. The cow path wiggled ahead, down to the stepping-stones, and all the way home. They followed it, and they talked.

Father must have been thinking of this trip, and that she might feel lonely. He said that God planned for His children to have lonesome times. Look at Abraham, moving from place to place and never really belonging anywhere. Everybody else worshiped idols. He walked alone with God! Father said God was especially near to those who dare to walk alone with Him.

Look at Joseph, in prison for years and years. It wasn't his fault. He hadn't done anything wrong at all. But God was preparing him to be governor of Egypt! Look at Moses who led the people of Israel for 40 years. Israel often grumbled and even threatened to stone him to death.

Father said it was that way with Christians. All the really great ones came to depend on God and not on people.

They had come to the stepping-stones. Sarah could see the place where she herded cattle that day. Suddenly she wanted to tell him all about it. So she did. She told him how lonesome she felt—lonesome as the sparrow on the housetop, or a pelican in the wilderness—the way the Bible says. So lonesome, she wanted to run away!

"Ah!" said Father. "And why was that? Were you lonely because you were doing what God wanted you to do?"

She shook her head. "I was running away from Him, I guess," she said.

"That's a different kind of loneliness," said Father.

"That's the kind we bring upon ourselves. Like the prodigal son. God has many runaways."

"Like—Keith?" Sarah asked.

"Yes," her father answered.

Sarah wondered then—should she ask him about it, or shouldn't she? At the wedding she heard those men talking. It was when they spoke about the *tame* wedding.

She glanced up at Father—glanced away—and back at him again.

He smiled. She could see his teeth gleaming. "Well, what is your decision?" he said. "Will you tell—or won't you?"

"Tell what?" said Sarah, startled.

"I don't know. But obviously there's something on your mind."

They were climbing the hill now, hand in hand, matching their footsteps.

"Well?" said Father.

"It's sort of mixed up," Sarah began. "It's about something that happened at Kathleen's wedding. They said, I mean that old Mr. Cavendish said, that you and Mother used to be gay as anything. The life of the party, is what he said. He said religion had—had *soured* you. He said— No, it was another man who said that you had spoiled all of us—all except Keith. He said Keith was the only one of us that had any—any— Is *gupshon* a word, Father?"

"Gumption, perhaps?"

"Yes. Gumption. What does it mean?"

"I suppose you could say it means the ability to see what needs to be done—and the initiative to do it. Do you know what *initiative* means?"

"Well, *sort* of—" said Sarah a bit doubtfully. "Well, and then someone laughed and said, 'So Keith lit out—with a neighborly assist—' "

Father's hand suddenly squeezed hers so hard that it hurt. He hadn't meant to. His voice remained calm.

"And then?" he asked.

"Well, that was all. I guess someone saw me. I guess I shouldn't have been listening. I was supposed to be carrying platefuls of cookies and things. Someone said that thing about little pitchers having big ears. *You* know."

Father chuckled a bit. For once he didn't lecture her for listening to gossip though. What he said was "And do you agree that your mother and I are sour people, Princess?"

"No! Oh, no!" she exclaimed.

"Well, thank you!" he said, and he laughed.

Then he answered some of her questions. He and Mother were not Christians when they were married. They *thought* they were having a good time. But since coming to know Jesus they knew better. They had found happier and more worthwhile things to do. And they hoped and prayed that all their children would choose Jesus too.

"I have," whispered Sarah.

He squeezed her hand, and she squeezed back, and they were so happy! Just about then they came to the corral, so there wasn't time for more talk.

But today at the station it was Mother who worried about their being alone.

"Oh, John, have we made the wrong decision?" Sarah heard her ask. "What if something dreadful should happen to them while we're gone?

And Father said, "We were sure this was the Lord's will, Love. He will take care of them. It may help to remember they will be in school or asleep the greater part of the time—and that there are chores enough to keep them out of mischief the remaining hours. They're good responsible children, besides."

Good responsible children. The words gave her a warm feeling. It took away some of the lonesome ache. The Ford touring car purred on, swooping down into the hollows and climbing the hills sturdily. The light flickered still, but Sarah could sort of half see dry sloughs and leafless bushes as they scudded past. And, once, a pair of cat's eyes—twin green stars that blinked out suddenly.

Good responsible children. Father didn't know she was on the other side of the magazine rack when he said that. So that's what he really thought.

"Well, here we are," said Mr. Slocum. "Sarah Naomi? You awake?"

"Yes, Mr. Slocum." She hopped out, but she shivered just a bit in the night breeze. "Thanks for the ride, Mr. Slocum."

"You're very welcome, I'm sure," he said with his high tee-hee-hee laugh.

A light was burning in the kitchen. Stuart must be home from choir practice. Sarah was glad she and Robbie needn't walk into a dark, empty house.

When bedtime came, she could choose. Mother had said she might sleep in their bedroom if she wished. That bed had a real mattress! And it had coil springs that creaked and twanged when you turned. It was interesting to sleep on. But—Robbie and Stuart would be upstairs. Of course, she wasn't *scared*. Not really scared. But their room seemed awfully far away when you were downstairs all alone in the dark.

Stuart had hot cocoa waiting tonight. And Mother had baked cinnamon rolls this morning. They each had a cupful of cocoa and one roll, sitting close to the warm stove. Then Stuart filled the firebox with coal and closed all the drafts, and they went upstairs.

It's funny. Sometimes when you feel the saddest you act the silliest. This evening Sarah had left her door open just a crack for company, and Stuart and Robbie left theirs open too. And they began a favorite game, making up nonsense poetry, each thinking up a line in turn. It kept getting funnier and funnier. So, giggling, Sarah fell asleep at last.

Mornings were the hardest to face. The bed felt so cozy and Mother wasn't there to make sure Sarah and Robbie got up in time. Stuart did his best, but he had to leave early for Blakely each morning. One day he just plain gave up. They had been reading a bit late the evening before. He called six times. He told them so later. Each time they grunted—and went right back to sleep.

When Sarah awoke the sun was high—and the house was quiet. It sent funny prickles through her. She jumped up and scampered downstairs in her nightgown.

The kitchen was cold. The firebox was open. The fire was out! Ashes were strewn all over the top of the stove. There were dirty dishes on the table. Sarah raced to the window. The top buggy was gone! She raced to the living room to peek at the clock. It was 8:30! Oh, wowie!

"Robbie! Robbie!" she shrieked up the stairs.

Say, that brought him thundering down in a hurry!

They'd be late to school today. Even if they hurried as fast as they could, and if they went without breakfast, they'd be late. You can't just go without milking, and feeding the calves and chickens, and slopping the pigs. They're live animals. They mustn't suffer.

Robbie was shrugging into his jacket. "Stuart milked. See? The separator's been used. So I'll feed the calves and chickens and things. You hurry and pack our lunch. And don't forget to get dressed!" he shouted as he slammed the door behind him. He was hurrying so fast that he slopped some milk on the floor.

It was a good thing Father had cut Sarah's hair short before he left home. She could take care of it alone now. She dressed and washed and whipped the brush through her tangles. She made bread-and-butter sandwiches and cut some cheese. She tumbled the things into the two syrup pails they used to carry their lunches. She raced down to the cellar for some apples. And she slammed the lids of the pails down with her fists just as Robbie and Wally came trotting up to the garden gate.

Some of Mother's cinnamon rolls were left. She grabbed a few and they ate them on the way to school. Robbie persuaded Wally that he'd better shake a leg. So they were only about half an hour late.

But Sarah had never been late in all her life before! Walking into a schoolroom when everyone turns to stare at you is hard. She felt ashamed, and she felt like crying. And when they got back home that evening, all the mess was waiting just the way they left it.

But they worked hard. When Stuart came home from

Blakely they had a fire blazing in the stove. The floor was swept and mopped. The top of the stove was wiped clean. Sarah was setting the table. She knew how to bake biscuits and fry potatoes, so that was what they were going to have. Stuart could fry eggs if he wanted to.

"Well!" he said, and he looked around. Then he smiled slowly, and they grinned back at him, feeling sheepish.

"After this," said Stuart, "certain people whose names I might mention but won't—certain people are going to go to bed on time, and they're going to get up when called in the morning. Right?"

Robbie sighed. "You better believe we will. Whew! I don't want another morning like we had today."

But Saturdays were different. Mrs. Slocum did the laundry and the baking for them. She'd do it on Fridays while they were in school. She even mopped the floors, which she wasn't expected to. So Saturdays seemed to stretch out before them. The chores had to be done—but they had so much time to do them! The hours just sort of slid along. And it might be 4 o'clock before the beds were made, and evening before the breakfast dishes got washed.

"Know something, Stuart?" said Sarah ruefully the second Saturday night. "You ought to *make* Robbie and me do our chores properly, at the right time." He was drying dishes for her, but she had to do the washing. He said they were too crusty for him and took too much scraping. "You ought to *boss* us more."

"Oh, I should, should I?" he said. "And what's wrong with you learning to boss yourselves? I have to study hard all Saturday to make up for lost time. About time you two became responsible."

Responsible. *Good responsible children* was what Father called them.

Sarah sighed. She and Robbie just fooled away most of today. And it wasn't a happy way to live. But bossing yourself was harder than being bossed.

"Look," said Stuart. "It might help if—if all of us remembered that Jesus is interested in the way we do things every day—in how faithful we are." Stuart was sort of shy about some things. Talking like this wasn't easy for him.

But Sarah was glad he did. "Let's have singing tonight," she begged. "It'll seem more like home."

Sarah could chord on the organ—key of C—if you didn't sing too fast. Stuart had Louise Thatcher's guitar at home, and he could strum it pretty well, with fancy runs and everything. So they sang. And then, for the first time, Stuart led evening devotions, just like Father. Then they had their baths in the kitchen, just like always. And then they went to bed.

But Sarah prayed silently even then. *Dear Lord Jesus, help me not to fool away the time. Help me to be good and responsible.*

But it still wasn't easy to get up in the mornings. She simply had to do it whether she felt like it or not.

It would be wonderful, she thought, if she could hear the Lord's voice saying, *Get up. Get dressed. Set the breakfast table. Wash the dishes*— And each time there'd be a little engine inside, or something, that would start up, and make her do the right thing in the right way. Why, she'd never make any mistakes anymore!

Robbie and Stuart didn't think much of the idea when she told them.

"Huh, who's always grumbling that people are too bossy?" hooted Robbie. "You'd feel the same way if you had to do what the Lord told you to."

"Besides," added Stuart, "He wants us to serve Him because we want to, because we love Him, not because we can't help it. He doesn't want any puppets."

"Well, but—" sighed Sarah.

If only it wouldn't be so much easier to do wrong things than right things! It was the easiest thing to forget to read the Bible and to pray in the mornings. It was hard to do as the Bible said, even when she understood what the verses meant. "Love your enemies," for instance. She didn't have *real* enemies, of course. But when people made fun of her she didn't feel much like loving them.

She used to think that if she'd be a Christian she'd have no more bothers. But no such thing! Sometimes it seemed as if there were two of her. One Sarah Scott wanted to please the Lord—truly wanted to. The other was interested only in doing and saying the things that Sarah Naomi wanted to do and say.

So why couldn't the Lord have made things easier?

On Wednesday morning of that third week, for instance—

If Mother had been at home she would have made Sarah and Robbie dress properly. The sun was shining, but a north wind blew. Yesterday everyone wore jackets and sweaters to school. They didn't want to be the only ones with winter things on! So she and Robbie shivered most of the way to school. Their fingers and lips were blue with cold, and Sarah's hand could hardly grasp the pencil all through the first period. And every single other pupil wore a coat or windbreaker to school that day.

After a bit, the sun disappeared altogether. The wind really blew chill now. After school Sarah and Robbie lingered a while so none of the other pupils could watch them leave, but they hurried to get away then before Miss Haliday was ready to go.

And now both of them were shielding their faces as well as they could. Before they were halfway home Sarah was crying silently, the tears turning to ice on her cheeks.

"Here, take my jacket," said Robbie roughly.

But she shook her head. "J-just m-make W-Wally go f-faster," she sobbed.

They had a coarse wool blanket over their knees, two thicknesses of it. Robbie stopped Wally, and he shook out the blanket, and tucked part around her. That helped some. But her knees and legs were colder now.

And when they arrived at home the fires were out, and the house felt like Aunt Jane's icehouse.

"Don't *cry!*" said Robbie impatiently now. "Give me time to get the fire going!"

"I'm n-not really crying," sobbed Sarah. "It's j-just th-that I c-can't st-stop!"

When Stuart came home, he sent her straight to bed. In Father and Mother's bed. He put a hot-water bottle at her feet. And he made her drink two cupsful of hot milk. After a bit she stopped shaking. She felt herself dropping off to sleep. The last thing she heard was Stuart saying gloomily, "Well, guess that does it. She'll be sick, and I'll have to miss school. And we have two tests coming up tomorrow."

That night the snow came.

CHAPTER 8

October Blizzard

SARAH AWOKE, her nose twitching. A lovely smell. Oh, mothballs!

She opened her eyes and looked around the room in surprise. How ever did she get *here?* Then, bit by bit, she remembered— The cold, cold drive. The icy house. Robbie trying to cut kindling, his hands all stiff from the cold. Stuart coming home, worried as anything about her.

She felt fine now. She felt *wonderful.* The bed was cozy as anything, and the coil springs twanged gently when she moved ever so slightly. Piled on top of her was Grandmother Murray's old feather bed—the one she brought from Ontario when Mother was a little girl. So that's where the mothball smell came from. Stuart must *really* have been worried about her. The thought made her feel important.

Next she noticed that the morning light looked strange. So *white.* She slid from the bed— Ouch! The floor was so cold it almost burned her soles. But she ran to the window on tiptoes for a quick look.

Snow. Why, the whole garden lay under a feather bed this morning. Snow was still coming down in slanting streaks from the north. This room was on the south side, so that was why she couldn't hear the wind. She scampered back to bed, and tucked the feather bed around her shoulders again.

Snow. First she thought, *Goody!* Then she thought, *Oh, dear!*

Whatever would they do about going to school?

The shafts would have to be changed over from the buggy to the sleigh. And there wouldn't be time before school today. So what were they going to do?

She could hear Stuart getting the fires started now. Then he peered cautiously into the room. At sight of her cheerful grin, part of the worried look slid from his face. But he still had problems.

Getting the big bobsled ready wouldn't take much time. All they had to do was move the box from the wagon to the sled. So he or Robbie could use that, with Prince and Captain hitched to it. And the other could ride Hyacinthe.

"But we can't leave you at home alone. So we were wondering—how would you like to stay with Mrs. Slocum today? No? Why not?"

For Sarah's face had grown longer and longer. Mrs. Slocum was a nice lady. Mother always said she had a heart as big as the world. Look at the way she organized things at threshingtime. But she had such a booming voice that any house she was in always seemed too crowded.

"I'd rather stay at home alone. But why can't I go to school?" Sarah asked.

"Well, you can't, and that's that!" Stuart told her.

"Mother would let me—I *think*."

"If Mother had been here, you wouldn't have done such a foolish thing as to go to school in that thin sweater. So you wouldn't have been so chilled. Besides, she knows more about sicknesses than I do. I'm not going to risk it."

In the end, Robbie stayed at home, and Stuart took the bobsled. They watched him drive away. But the snow was tumbling down so fast now, the sled was out of sight before it reached the road.

There's something exciting about a first snowfall. Robbie went to the woodshed and brought great armfuls of wood—thin pieces and great big chunks. He filled the woodbox and piled more armloads on the floor along the wall. He found a heap of coal left over from last year too, and he brought in a scuttleful of that. They'd be able to keep a fire going all night. Next, he went to the well for a pailful of water. It was snowing so hard that a thick blanket of slush was floating on top when he came back.

He wouldn't let Sarah step outdoors to help with any of this. But he wouldn't dry a single dish for her. That was girl's work. That's the way things would be in his house when he grew up and got married!

They had fun. It was like a storybook, where the hero and heroine are in a stockade, getting ready for a siege. You keep watch through the little holes in the walls to see if the enemy is sneaking up on you. Only this time the enemy was snow. And it couldn't do a single thing to hurt them—not if it tried ever so!

The wind made a good draft in the chimney, and the fires chewed over the chunks of wood, groaning a bit, and the house was snug as anything.

Robbie and Sarah did homework, working ahead in arithmetic and spelling and literature. Robbie drilled Sarah in geography too—which country exported what. (That was dreadful stuff.) And then they cut families out of an old Eaton's catalog, and pasted them onto cardboard so they could stand up. And they cut out clothes for all the people. It's really tricky to find clothes that are the right size and that are *all there*, with no sleeve or part of the trousers missing.

"But don't you dare tell in school what we did," said Robbie fiercely.

Sarah giggled. "I'll tell them you played paper dolls with me!"

"If you dare! I'll—I'll—"

But he never finished saying what dreadful things he would do in return. Just that minute Sarah thought she heard a scratching sound at the door. She ran to see. Spencer! He was begging to come indoors! Why, he practically never wanted to step over the sill. The only time he did, usually, was during a thunderstorm. Now he padded in and curled up in front of the stove.

"Hey, Spencer, old boy!" With his fingers Robbie combed the snow out of his tan and silver coat. Then he wiped him carefully with old rags.

Sarah had to step over and around him while heating up yesterday's stew (it got only a *little* scorched) and while mixing and baking biscuits. But that was all right. She liked having her friend so close.

After dinner Robbie left the dishwashing all to Sarah again. He said importantly that he had to check on the stock in the barn. The yearlings would be all right. They had already begun eating their way into the enormous strawstack. They did it each fall and winter. When the snowy winds came they went on eating—and made rooms and passages all through the stack. It was a warm shelter in winter—and a lovely hide-and-seek place in summer.

The cows were in the barn though.

After Robbie went out, Sarah did the dishes. Then she thought she had better sweep up some of the mess on the floor, and she giggled again. She wouldn't *really* tell about Robbie cutting paper dolls, but she could pretend she was going to. It would be fun to tease him and keep him guessing.

She could hear him stamping snow off his boots on the porch now. Then he almost tumbled into the kitchen. There was a half-scared look on his face.

"It's Coral. She—she's acting funny."

Sarah clapped her hand to her mouth. Above it her eyes grew enormous. "Not her baby calf getting born!"

"I'm not sure. But I'm afraid so," said Robbie.

And here it was, about 1:30. Stuart wouldn't be home before five.

"We'll have to pray that it won't be born so quick," said Sarah, cheering up. You could pray about anything. That was one nice thing about belonging to God.

The wind kept getting stronger though, that was the trouble. Robbie prowled from window to window. Wherever you looked there was this moving wall of white. If you stood at the north window you could barely see the jutting peak of the barn roof now.

"Know something?" said Sarah, peering over his shoulder. "We ought to tie a rope between here and the barn."

"Be a good idea," agreed Robbie. "*If* we had a rope."

"We do! Don't you remember? Father bought that long thin rope in summer to make a short thick one for—I don't remember. What was it for? *Anyway,* it's hanging in the woodshed right this minute."

So Robbie had to go out again. Both of them felt better after the rope was in place because the wind grew worse and the snow kept tumbling out of the skies.

Coral wasn't any worse, Robbie reported after his last trip. But she wasn't any better. She seemed dreadfully restless, as if she couldn't make up her mind to lie down or remain standing. She acted mad at him too. Maybe she was all right. He just didn't know!

Oh, if Stuart would only come!

The telephone bell made a whispering sound, a faint, faint ringing. Sarah strained to hear. Two longs—two shorts— Was that it?

"Hello?" she said, just to make sure. "Hello?"

There was a dreadful hum on the wires. She thought she heard Stuart's voice. But the words were far away. They sounded like "gobble-gabble-gubble-ubble." And then silence. The line went dead.

Robbie snatched the receiver from her hand. He listened. He shouted "hello" over and over. He tried ringing Central. It wasn't any use. The line was dead. The wind must have tangled some wires.

When Robbie swung around, his face looked like an old man's face, tight and wrinkled with worry. "Why didn't you let *me* talk with him? Now—"

"You wouldn't have heard any better!" snapped Sarah. "I have very good ears. Father says so!"

Robbie couldn't have felt like arguing today. He changed the subject. "Know what I think? I think Stuart phoned to say he'd have to stay in town. There's that ravine. It gets choked something fierce in a snowstorm."

Sarah's knees felt rubbery all of a sudden. She dropped into the nearest chair, and clasped her hands tight—and stared at Robbie.

He didn't help matters. "I'm—plain—scared," he said.

So was Sarah. Oh, so was she! But what was there for them to do?

"I—I think I'm going to have to ride to Slocum's—" Robbie said.

"Telephone!" began Sarah. But, of course—*that* was no good.

She swallowed, and she could hear her throat squeak.

"Tell you what," said Robbie. "Let's have supper now. Just anything—with hot cocoa. It's going to be a cold ride."

And dangerous. But he didn't mention that.

"There's some of Mrs. Slocum's pie left," said Sarah bravely.

She remembered other leftovers. Cold boiled potatoes. She fried them and added two eggs just at the last. She and Robbie liked them that way. And they had some cold biscuits and the apple pie and cocoa.

Usually when the two of them ate alone they just thought their prayer silently. Today Robbie surprised Sarah. He prayed right out—and he asked God to keep Stuart safe—and to bring him and Hyacinthe safe to Slocum's and back. Amen.

"And, dear Lord," added Sarah, "don't let anything serious happen to Coral. She's a purebred cow and cost an awful lot of money. And Father would feel dreadful if things went wrong. So don't let them, please. Thank You. Amen."

They felt better after that.

All the same, Sarah had a strange scary feeling when Robbie walked out of the house this time. Almost before he reached the gate she lost sight of him. The storm just seemed to swallow him whole.

She washed the dishes and swept the floor again. She lit the lamp because the room was almost dark now. Then she put more wood on the fire. Then there wasn't a single other job she could think to do.

So she tried to play the organ— And she tried to play with her Kathleen doll—and she took up *Swiss Family Robinson* to read a bit— She simply was too restless for anything. By now Robbie had been gone a whole hour. It was only a half mile to Slocums.

Spencer was no help. He had begun to whine and pace the floor. Every once in a while he would stop beside Sarah and lick her hand anxiously. She put her arms around his neck and buried her face in his silky ruff. And together they listened to the rising howl of the wind.

Dear Jesus— Sarah was praying in her heart. *Bring Robbie safely home. Don't let him be lost in the snow.*

Tears trickled down her cheeks to get lost in Spencer's ruff. Suddenly, he pulled away from her. He whined urgently now, and padded to the door and pointed his nose at the knob.

She spoke to him in a frightened whisper, begging him to stay. But, it seemed he just had to go out in the storm.

So Sarah opened the door. The collie disappeared into the black and white night.

Sarah sat at the table, with her head on the crook of her arm, staring into the flame of the lamp. Every thought was a prayer now. *Keep him safe. Bring him back. Let Mr. Slocum come with him—*

Suddenly she heard barks. And voices! There was a thumping sound at the door. She raced to the door and tore it open. She peered into the dark entry just as the other door opened. Two snowmen came slithering in, waving their arms to keep from sprawling all over the floor! The dry snow under their boots was dangerous on the ice-cold linoleum of the entry. Their faces were plastered with more snow, and they were panting and blowing as if they had run for miles.

"Dog—saved—our—lives—shouldn't wonder—" gasped the bigger snowman.

"Thought—we were—lost," mumbled the smaller one through stiff lips. "Then—heard bark—"

Mr. Slocum stripped off his mitts and shook his hands in the air to warm them a bit. Robbie had plunked down on a chair, all of him heaving at each breath. Spencer sat at his feet, just looking into his face lovingly, and waving his snowy tail slowly.

Coral was getting along all right. They had just stopped at the barn long enough to look at her and put the tired horses into their stalls.

"Boy, you should see the drifts between here and Slocum's!" said Robbie, as he gulped a cup of cocoa that Sarah had rewarmed.

Then Robbie and Mr. Slocum went out again. But this

time Spencer was quite content to stay with Sarah. And she wasn't worried now. The guide rope was up. After a bit Robbie came back in—for the washtub!

"Whatever for?" Sarah asked.

"We're bringing the calf in. He's pretty weak," Robbie said. "And the barn is draughty tonight."

So that was how it came about that Sarah and Spencer sat beside the tub a bit later, looking at just the wettest, slickest, most shivery calf you ever saw. Sarah wondered if he had any hair at all. But then Mr. Slocum came indoors again, and he began rubbing the little fellow gently with an old towel.

"Wait till his ma gets him all dressed up with her rough tongue. He'll be real purty then. Takes a cow's tongue to put the right ripple in a calf's head and neck hair, and the right curl in his tail. What you goin' to name him?"

It would be a fancy name, all right. For everyday they might call him Rex. Something short and *useful*. But he'd have a real birth certificate, just like people. Because he was an important calf, a purebred. His name would hint at who his parents and grandparents were. That's how important he was!

He looked so tiny now, and for a while it seemed he had hardly any voice. But suddenly he let out a bawl that startled Sarah.

"Ready to go back to his ma," said Mr. Slocum, grinning.

When the excitement was over, Sarah Naomi remembered she had a problem. Where to put Mr. Slocum for the night? She didn't think Robbie would want him to sleep in Stuart's bed. So she changed sheets in Father and

Mother's bed as well as she could. (It was a good thing Susan's ma wasn't watching!) It was the warmest room anyway, being so close to the kitchen and living room stoves.

When Robbie and Mr. Slocum came back indoors, the living room clock was bing-bonging, announcing that it was 10 o'clock.

But—Mr. Slocum wasn't sleepy!

You can't simply go to bed and leave your guest sitting in the kitchen. Robbie perched on the woodbox, one knee drawn up to his chin. Sarah sat at the table, her head pillowed on both arms. Looking past the lamp she could see Mr. Slocum sitting, long and thin, with his shoulders stooped, and his long fingers between his knees. It was when she noticed the twinkle in his eyes that Sarah felt a tiny prickle of fear.

Mr. Slocum did a lot of traveling, buying and selling horses and cattle. So he could tell the most interesting stories. He was a kind man too—usually. But when he began asking teasing questions he was the only one who had fun. Usually.

Tonight he wanted to know all about how she felt and acted while Robbie was gone today. "So then even Spencer deserted you! You wasn't afraid, eh? Don't tell me you was afraid! Eh? Eh?"

Thump-thump went Sarah's heart. "Yes, I was," she said soberly.

"You *was?* You don't say! What did you do? Crawl under the bed to hide?"

Sarah shook her head slightly. Her heart was fluttering right on her tongue now. She swallowed it. "I—I prayed."

CHAPTER 9

Eight Toes—and a Welcome

AFTERWARD SARAH NAOMI WONDERED— Why did Mr. Slocum ask all those questions? Was he only teasing? Or did he really want to know?

About the Bible. About how to become a Christian. About family devotions.

"Come now, Sarah Naomi. You say you're a Christian. Now me, I guess I'm a heathen, pretty near. Ain't it your duty to learn me? What's this here family devotion thing?"

She had thought that maybe she and Robbie could have a thanksgiving prayer together—later. Because God had answered their prayers and kept them safe and helped Coral's calf to be born and everything. You don't pray that kind of a prayer just to show that you can!

Sarah looked pleadingly across the room at Robbie. He slid suddenly from his perch on the woodbox and went to get the big Bible. Maybe he thought this was one way to hurry bedtime along.

"I'll *read*," he said quietly to her.

That meant *And you do the praying*.

100

Robbie opened the Bible where the marker was. When he began reading, Sarah started, she was so surprised. He was reading about them—about today—here and now!

This was what she heard:

> Oh that men would praise the Lord for his goodness, and for his wonderful works to the children of men! . . . Such as sit in darkness and in the shadow of death, . . . they fell down, and there was none to help. Then they cried unto the Lord in their trouble, and he saved them out of their distresses. . . . Oh that men would praise the Lord.

It was true as true! God did help them out of their distresses. Sarah was only a bit afraid of praying aloud with Mr. Slocum to hear her.

For about a half minute after she was through, the room was very quiet. Outside the wind howled. And the fire still whined over its chunks of wood. But Sarah could hear Mr. Slocum breathing. There was no twinkle in his eyes now.

He cleared his throat. "Who's this here absent loved one you was prayin' for so special?"

"It's Keith. We pray for him every day. Especially Father," she said softly.

"Oh?" he said.

"It's like the Bible story. You remember about the runaway boy? He went into a far country. But every day his father kept watching for him, hoping he'd come home. And he did! One day he really did! He was ragged as anything, and half starved. But the father knew him 'while he was yet a great way off'—that's what the Bible says. And he hugged and kissed him, and he made a feast for him—and—"

Her eyes caught Robbie's. They held a warning look. *Why?*

"And then?" said Mr. Slocum.

"I—I guess it's time to go to bed, Mr. Slocum. It's 11 o'clock!"

For there was the living room clock—bing-bonging away again.

So they filled the stoves and closed the dampers and went to bed.

For a long time though, Sarah couldn't sleep. Her room was icy cold, so she curled into a ball and she breathed under the covers to help warm her little nest.

First she thought of Robbie, and the look he gave her across the table tonight. *You're talking too much,* it said. But why? If it wouldn't be so cold up here she'd go right this minute and ask him.

Then her thoughts swung to Stuart. In sudden fear she began whispering, "Dear Lord Jesus, keep him safe. We don't really know that he stayed in town. We're just guessing. Maybe he's out in this storm somewhere. You know where he is. Keep him safe. Bring him safe home."

All this time the wind roared and slammed around the corners of the house. It laid strong rough hands on the windows and shook them till the panes rattled. The world seemed awfully big and wild and lonesome tonight. Sarah pulled the comforter closer around her head, leaving only a tiny hole to breathe through. After a while she must have fallen asleep.

When she awoke next morning the storm was over. It was very cold still, and there was no sun. The yard was like an immense bowlful of whipped cream, with funny looking peaks and hollows all over the place. Mr. Slocum was gone. He got up early to start the fires so the house would warm up. Then he milked Coral and fed the calf. Then he rode home. Sarah could see where his horse had had to break through the wall of snow to get away.

For the second day in a row, Sarah and Robbie stayed home from school. Today wasn't as much fun as yesterday—nor as frightening. About 11 o'clock a rider came into the yard. They couldn't recognize his face. It was all muffled with a scarf, on account of the cold. But he kept staring up at the telephone wires. So they knew. It was Mr. Spinks, the telephone man. He was looking for breaks in the wire. He shoved the scarf from his mouth.

"You kids OK?" he shouted across the sea of drifts. "That'll relieve Stuart's mind. He was considerably worried about you, let me tell you."

"Is he all right?" Robbie called back.

"Sure, sure. Spent the night at our home. Wife and I had to do a tall lot of persuadin' though. He was bound and determined to ride home in all the storm."

Then they were alone again. A few minutes later the telephone gave a clinking sound. It worked again! Mr. Spinks must have found the trouble spot.

At noon two things happened. Stuart phoned. And Robbie milked Coral for the first time. It was not a success. The heifer didn't like it at all, and she had a swift kick. Over and over she knocked the pail aside, and Robbie along with it.

Sarah stood in the aisle, watching. And shivering. She wasn't cold. In fact, with all the horses in their stalls and the cows in their stanchions, the barn was warm and moist. It smelled pleasantly of oats and hay and other barn smells.

"She'll hurt you! She'll really hurt you!" said Sarah.

"Well, but—" puffed Robbie. He was all out of breath from being knocked down so often. "The calf has to be fed." There were tears on his cheeks. He tried to hide them, and Sarah pretended she hadn't noticed.

"Couldn't you let the calf suck—just this once?" she asked.

It might cause trouble later on. But they shut him in with his ma and left them together there. Maybe Stuart could handle the heifer.

About 3 o'clock two bobsleds came into the yard. Mr. Darnley and Mr. Slocum were driving them. They were breaking trail, driving back and forth, back and forth, to pack the snow down. Mr. Slocum remembered to stop long enough to change the shafts from the buggy to the old school sleigh. Robbie and Sarah would be able to go to school tomorrow.

When Stuart came home they proudly showed him the surprise in the barn. And then they had so much talking to do—all the stories about the Great October Blizzard to tell and hear. Sarah could hardly tear herself away. But she had supper to cook.

Cocoa again. And toast. The bread was pretty dry anyway. She had forgotten to cover the bread box properly. And applesauce. And scrambled eggs. They weren't really intended to be scrambled, but when Sarah fried eggs they usually turned out that way. Robbie groaned when he saw them. Stuart went down into the cellar for a jar of pickles and one of home-canned meat.

They talked and laughed a lot, fooling around. But the happiest thought was that Mother and Father would be back next week. Sarah thought, *Only seven more suppers to cook!*

Two nights later they all had a surprise.

Sarah awoke out of a deep sleep. She heard a sound and thought she must be dreaming. Water trickling, trickling down the rainspouts! She bounded out of bed. But the room was still very dark, and she ran to raise the window shade. The snow on the sill was wet and mushy. The air coming in smelled wet too.

Springtime in October! It was the strangest feeling.

Stuart rode Hyacinthe to Blakely that morning. Sarah and Robbie used the sleigh.

Sarah had a problem this morning. The road would be wet and the school yard slushy. She would need rubbers. Every day now the whole of Braeburn school played prisoner's base. The game went on and on—it was so exciting! She couldn't miss it. But, she couldn't wear the rubbers over her school sandals. Last winter's felt boots fit into the rubbers nicely but the felt was torn at places. Six of her toes poked through the holes. She would just have to wear the rubbers all day. The Siddons always did in wet weather, so that was all right.

Last winter's coat seemed to have shrunk an awful lot. The sleeves especially. But it had a lovely mothball smell. Sarah went to school quite happily. How was she to know that this was the day when Miss Haliday would make a new rule?

NO RUBBERS ARE TO BE WORN IN THE SCHOOL-ROOM. She announced it, and she wrote it in large letters on the board so all would know and remember.

Sarah Naomi's heart skittered. *I can't take my rubbers off,* she thought. *And I can't tell why. I'd be ashamed to.*

After recess she came in by the rear door. She walked carefully so her rubbers wouldn't squeak. Teacher made sure the Siddons wore no rubbers. She never thought to check Sarah's feet.

If only Teacher doesn't call up our class, thought Sarah. Teacher didn't. And all that period Sarah kept her feet tucked under her desk.

Then, at the end, Susan Gerrick had to go and spoil things.

Sarah's thoughts were far away. With Heidi and Peter she was herding goats in the Swiss mountains and valleys. This was one of the lovely stories in her grade four reader. Suddenly she felt a jab. Her eyes focused slowly on Susan's round worried face.

"Rubbers!" she whispered, pointing. "Rubbers!"

There was nothing wrong with Miss Haliday's ears.

"Sarah Naomi, go into the hall this minute. And come back without your rubbers."

Sarah sat. She felt as if someone had poured glue all over her seat and the floor under her desk. She couldn't take off her rubbers. She simply couldn't.

"Sarah! This minute!" Miss Haliday had never used that tone to Sarah Scott before.

Slowly she turned. Slowly she got to her feet, and she walked up the aisle to Teacher's desk.

"Please," she whispered. "Please let me wear them!"

Miss Haliday drew her head back. She couldn't believe her ears! That's what her face said. What her lips said was "Go to the hall. Take off your rubbers. Don't let me have to repeat again! And remain at your desk at noon."

Shamed, Sarah turned to stumble down the aisle. Past Robbie's desk. His face was almost buried in his book, but his neck had flushed a dark red. Past Susan. She looked worried and sorry. Some grinned at Sarah, happy because someone was miserable. Some made faces at Teacher behind their books.

Even when the door closed behind her, Sarah's trouble wasn't over. Off came the rubbers. Out came *eight* bare toes! Two more than this morning.

Bare feet in warm weather are all right. Most of Braeburn pupils went barefoot. But bare toes are shameful. And when they poke out of torn black stockings they look awfully lonesome, somehow. Sarah leaned against a cluster of coats and wished she dared to run away home.

"Sarah Naomi!" called Teacher firmly.

She had to walk back in. Most of the heads swiveled around. Snickers broke out, and then came a wave of laughter.

Sarah held up her head as she marched to her seat. She couldn't see clearly, but she didn't cry—not until she felt Miss Haliday's hand on her head and heard her say,

"I'm sorry, Sarah. I might have known you would not deliberately disobey without a cause." Then her voice grew firm. "Hush, class. And if anyone dares to tease Sarah—!"

No one did. Some of the big girls coaxed her to come out and play as usual. She didn't have to remain at her desk after all. Outdoors she could wear her rubbers. She was a good runner, so she brought four prisoners home,

and she caught five enemies! So the day wasn't really ruined.

It wasn't over yet. That afternoon, about 3 o'clock, someone knocked on the schoolhouse door. All pupils hushed while Teacher went into the entry. She came back in with a strange look on her face.

"Sarah Naomi—Robbie—you are wanted. Better take your books with you."

Out in the cloakroom stood Father and Mother. Mother's arms were closing around Sarah when she noticed the eight sprouts on Sarah's feet.

"Oh, my poor waif!" she wailed in a whisper.

But Father shook with silent laughter most of the way home. Every once in a while he sobered enough to ask questions. About how they managed to do the chores. About the day they were late to school. About the coming of the storm, and of Coral's new calf. But whenever he thought of Sarah's feet, she could tell. His cheeks bulged, and there he was again, shaking his shoulders.

"Father! Don't!" pleaded Sarah.

She was riding home through the slushy snow in the two-seater buggy with her parents. Robbie came bumping behind in the cutter. By tomorrow, if the weather remained mild, most of the snow would be gone again.

"I don't know," said Mother, "how I'm *ever* going to forgive myself. Leaving my children like that for a month!"

Sarah snuggled close. "But it wasn't quite a month. What happened? Why did you come back sooner?"

"Too soon?" said Father, teasing. Then he added, "Whoa there, Prince and Captain."

They were home.

Robbie heard Father's last question. "Too *soon!* Hooo! If I ever eat another plateful of Sarah's scrambled eggs, it will be too soon."

That wasn't fair, and Sarah was hurt. But only a little. She was glad Mother and Father were back. The news of the storm made them decide to come early.

That evening after supper she and Robbie acted silly, just plain silly. They chased each other upstairs and downstairs, outdoors and back indoors again.

"Come and sit down, do," invited Father. "What makes you behave like this?"

Sarah threw up her arms and danced around the

kitchen. "We don't have to be *responsible* anymore!" she said, laughing.

Father couldn't help smiling. "Oh, *don't* you?" he said. "We'll see about that!"

But Mother said, "Let's go to the parlor for some singing."

So they did.

CHAPTER 10

Sarah Turns Detective

A FEW DAYS AFTER COMING HOME Mother had a long serious talk with Sarah. About obedience and respect to teachers. (On account of the rubbers!) And the next day she invited Miss Haliday down to tea.

A teacher's tea was a really elegant thing. Usually. To-day, Sarah's heart thumped as she saw Miss Haliday's palomino pony come prancing up the lane. Mother hadn't mentioned the word *apologize*. All the same, Sarah guessed that was what this tea was about.

It didn't turn out exactly that way though.

Mother stood waiting on the porch. Sarah stood in the entry behind her, soberly pressing her nose against the screen door. Miss Haliday came up the walk. She was smiling but in a timid sort of way. Miss Haliday!

"Mrs. Scott," she began immediately, "about that episode last week, I really must apologize—"

"No, no, Miss Haliday," said Mother. "You were quite within your rights. Quite. I've been a teacher too, you know. I can imagine how your sense of smell has been assaulted in the past."

"The Siddons tribe—" Teacher shook her head, wrinkling her nose. "But *your* child—"

Suddenly both ladies were rocking with laughter.

"—airing her toes like that—" shrieked Mother.

"—and her coat reeking of mothballs—" hooted Miss Haliday.

"—sleeves scarcely covering her elbows—" added Mother.

They were holding onto each other, laughing like anything. It really wasn't all that funny.

"But all the same," said Miss Haliday, wiping her eyes, "all the same I should have trusted Sarah. Mrs. Scott, she has never before failed to yield instant obedience— Oh, there you are, Sarah, I'm—I'm sorry."

Mother tucked her hanky behind her belt. She said briskly. "How about getting out Great-grandmother Murray's tea service, Sarah?"

It was very special silver. Mother inherited it because she was named after her grandmother. But she almost never used it. She said it didn't really belong on a Western farm.

Sarah lifted it carefully from the top shelf of the sideboard. She watched Mother brew the tea in the silver pot. And she filled the sugarbowl and cream jug. Then they moved to the parlor where the other tea things waited. It was elegant.

They nibbled fancy shortbread and sipped tea. Secretly, Sarah practiced curling her little finger just the way Miss Haliday did. And they talked. About Kathleen and Herbie, and the last news of how busy they were in school in far-off California. About Linda, and how her new doctor was really excited because she was improving so fast. He was trying new exercises on her. About Aunt Jane, who could walk with the help of a cane now. About places in Ontario that Mother and Father visited. Miss Haliday came from Ontario.

"You plan to return to your old home?" said Mother. "I believe I heard a rumor to that effect. Sarah, how about refilling Miss Haliday's cup?"

It was fun to watch the steaming brown liquid come out of the silver spout.

"Cream, Miss Haliday?" said Sarah politely.

Teacher had waited till now to answer Mother's question. "Well, yes—" she said slowly. Then, in a sort of rush, "That is, I had some thought— But plans change, you know." Miss Haliday was blushing!

"You are the first to know," she added, laughing. "I'll be following your example, it seems. In about two months I'll be marrying a local farmer."

Oh, no! thought Sarah. *Then there'll be no Miss Haliday in school!*

"Who is the fortunate man, if I may ask?" said Mother.

It was Grant Millar, Grace's bachelor brother! Mother looked surprised too. Grant Millar had a big farm, but he also had a big nose and bushy eyebrows. A lot of people laughed at him, he was so different. He was very quiet and seldom talked to anyone. But Grace said that he read loads of books, and knew all there was to know about birds and animals.

"He has the kindest heart in the world," said Miss Haliday, looking very happy.

"Well, I'm sure—" said Mother. "I'm sure we hope both of you will be very happy."

The wedding was to be in Miss Haliday's home in Ontario at Christmastime. After that she would come back to teach Braeburn till June. Grant thought it wouldn't be fair to the pupils to change teachers in the middle of the year, she said.

"But I hope, Sarah dear, you won't mind keeping a secret for me?"

Sarah said she wouldn't mind, and she felt proud to be trusted.

After tea, when she carried the tea things to the kitchen, Mother and Miss Haliday sat side by side talking in low serious voices. About Jesus? Sarah was almost sure. Miss Haliday belonged to a church back home. But she didn't seem to understand some things. That everybody needs Jesus because all are sinners—that we have to accept His forgiveness and be born again—

"Thank you, Mrs. Scott," she said when she was saying good-bye. "I'll think over what you've told me. Well, Sarah Naomi, am I forgiven?"

She sounded lively and happy again. Sarah never got around to apologizing for wearing the rubbers against the rule.

The engagement was to be *such* a secret. But before the week was over, all of Braeburn knew. Sarah never told. Someone must have.

One good thing was that Mother could invite all the Braeburn ladies now to a quilting bee! Each lady embroidered a square of white cloth with flowers and a "sentiment," a bit of poetry perhaps, or a Bible verse. Mother's "sentiment" was "In all thy ways acknowledge Him, and He shall direct thy paths."

It was the middle of November when the ladies came to do the quilting. Summer had returned! It was a steamy, sunny sort of day. Most of the trees were bare, except the evergreens, of course. But a lot of the bushes still carried their yellow and brown and scarlet leaves. The woods, when you passed them, had a lovely smell. Sharp. And perfumey. It made your nose curl with pleasure.

When Sarah and Robbie came home from school that day the yard was crammed with cars and buggies. As soon as she opend the house door—hooo! Sounds came gushing out to meet her. It was like a—like a *chicken house!* That's exactly how it sounded.

Of course, when you listened closely you could hear words. Mrs. Gerrick was telling Mrs. Darnley about her latest letter from Herbie and Kathleen. Mrs. Heathe was giving a cake recipe to the lady next to her. Mrs. Slocum was talking about her husband, and her voice could be heard best of all. All of them sat along the walls of the parlor, with the big quilt stretched taut between them. All were stitching away as fast as they talked.

But who was listening?

"So I says to him, I says—"

"Now take *me*, I always say—"

"Yes, two eggs, beaten separately—"

"Well, Slocum goes where he pleases. You won't catch me bossin' my man," boomed Mrs. Slocum. " 'Slocum', I says, 'if you wanted to be told what to do, you got yourself the wrong wife,' I says. He comes, he goes. Buyin' cattle and horses, sellin' 'em again. It keeps him happy—and he always makes a bit on the deals."

"Is he home now?" someone wanted to know.

"Yep," she answered. "Got back again two weeks ago. Sort of sudden, that last trip."

"Mother," whispered Sarah, tugging at her mother's sleeve, "I'm hungry. Could I have a roll?"

"We'll be serving lunch in a few minutes. As soon as the water boils," said Mother. "Can you wait?"

"Guess so," Sarah said.

It was pretty hard though. Most of the ladies had brought cake and cookies and sandwiches. Mother baked walnut-raisin-cinnamon rolls. They were cooling on the shelf in the pantry.

Sarah took another peek—just as a brown hand came sneaking over the sill, grabbed about six sugary rolls, and disappeared!

That Robbie Scott!

Sarah raced on tiptoes across the kitchen through the entry. She closed the outer door softly. If Robbie was going to the hayloft— But he didn't! She saw him walking rapidly now but innocently down the lane, whistling quietly. Then he crossed the road, took a quick look around, and ducked into the Heathe birch woods.

Well!

Sarah gave chase. Her sandals were silent on the driveway, and silent on the damp birch leaves. When she raced past the barn a while ago she could hear Spencer whining in there. Robbie must have penned him up. She had thought for a moment of freeing him. He'd be able to track Robbie in a hurry. But then she remembered he

would spoil the surprise. She was *really* going to startle Robbie this time. Greedy!

She was in the woods now, following a narrow winding path. Robbie had slowed a bit. Every now and then she could see him ahead of her. The white trunks of the trees, and the way the sunlight slanted through them, made it hard to follow his movements. But that was all right. He never once looked back, as far as she could tell. And this was the only path through these woods. Sarah knew it led to the old log cabin where Mr. Heathe lived before he was married. This land was his homestead.

But why didn't Robbie stop just anywhere to eat his rolls?

She was closer to him now. It was fun to dash silently from tree to tree—just in case he should turn around.

He didn't. When he came to the clearing he walked straight into the open and up to the log cabin. Its door, which had been torn from it hinges long ago, was propped into place now. He knocked. After a bit the door leaned outward a bit. And Robbie crawled under and into the cabin.

Sarah circled, stealing closer. The windows were stuffed with rags and old papers. On the east side there were two dusty little squares of glass left. When she climbed up to look in, she had to wait for her eyes to get used to the dark inside. And then all she saw was a wooden partition a few feet away!

She heard voices though. Robbie's—and another. She couldn't understand a word, but Robbie was talking to someone. Her hands grew tired of clutching the sill so she dropped to the ground again.

Should she march around and knock at the door? Maybe there was a gang of boys in there, and they would tease her for snooping. Besides, all that good food was waiting at home— By this time the ladies might be eating. And when Mrs. Gerrick and Mrs. Slocum and that other lady— What was her name? The big one from Blakely way— By the time they were through, there might not be much left!

Sarah was thinking so hard she was startled when she saw a long shadow moving beside her. Robbie coming! Quick as thought she darted around the other corner. He hadn't noticed. And he never looked back. He was hurrying home again.

If there hadn't been all those tea goodies waiting, Sarah would have gone to the cabin to investigate. *Maybe.* She wasn't really very brave. But she had a secret now—one that Robbie didn't want her to know. She couldn't tell if it was a happy one or not. She'd have to find out.

She trotted home rather soberly. Bits and pieces began clicking into place. Twice in the past two weeks a loaf of bread had disappeared from the bread box. At least, each time Mother was surprised to find out she had one loaf less than she thought she had. And now that Sarah thought of it, Robbie had been acting queer. He went walking a lot, and often he was moody and absentminded.

Once she heard Father say to Mother, "Well, after all, he is in his teens now. Growing up isn't easy. He'll have a lot of thinking to do."

"If only it's not the wrong kind of thinking," Mother said, sighing.

But a few days after that it was Father who got worried —and impatient.

"Robbie, it's one thing to go for a hike. But a dependable boy will be at home when there are chores to be done. Understand?"

Dependable. That was one of Father's favorite words.

So Robbie had been different, thought Sarah as she scooted up the hill from the creek. (She took the roundabout route so Robbie wouldn't guess she had been following him.) In school all the girls were excited about Miss Haliday's wedding, and about the surprise party they were planning. Perhaps that was why she hadn't noticed about Robbie before.

Oh, she hoped he wasn't in real trouble!

Should she tell Father and Mother? Not yet, she decided. Tomorrow was Saturday, and if the weather was nice again she could go back, maybe— If she could find out who was staying in that cabin—

* * *

The man sat on a tree stump in the clearing. He sat staring into the sunset when Sarah stole up behind him. He coughed every now and then. Between coughing spells he whistled quietly. Sarah was peeking out from behind a birch tree, but she might as well have stood out in the open. He hardly stirred at all. He had a big cowboy hat on his head, and it was pulled low over his eyes. Sarah thought he looked sad, but not dangerous—or—or scary.

Now he was whistling a song Sarah knew! "They say there will be a great roundup, when cowboys like dogies will stand. . . ." That was the cowboy way of talking about the great judgment, Sarah knew. She could whistle a bit, so she joined in.

You should have seen the way the man moved! Instantly

he was on his feet, facing her. His eyes searched the woods.

Sarah stood very still. She was half afraid now.

"Robbie?" he called softly. Sharply too. "Robbie, is that you?"

After waiting a bit Sarah couldn't stand the strain any longer. She stepped out.

"It's—it's not Robbie," she said, her heart hammering. "It's only me, Sarah Scott."

"So you are Sarah Naomi," he said softly.

"You know my *middle* name?" she exclaimed. "Did Robbie talk about me?"

"Yes, come to think of it, he must have," murmured the man.

He wasn't frightening in the least. His eyes were deep, and his shoulders sort of stooped. Otherwise he was about as big as Father. His name was Jack English, he said. And, yes, he'd been a real cowboy. He got chilled awhile back and couldn't seem to shake this cold. So he'd come to this cabin for a rest.

Sarah glanced at it, then quickly back at him. She didn't say what she was thinking. He must be *dreadfully* poor to have to stay in a junky place like the old Heathe cabin! But she didn't talk about poorness. It might shame him.

Instead, she chatted about things she did and about the family. About Herbie and Kathleen in California, and Stuart in grade 12 in high school—he was that smart!—about Father and Mother. She couldn't tell if he was interested. But she felt sorry for him, and didn't like to run away and leave him.

He sat tying fancy knots in a string.

"And is that the whole family?" he said.

"There's the absent loved one," said Sarah softly.

This was something you practically never discussed with strangers. But Mr. English looked sad, so maybe he'd understand. She told him about Keith, who ran away and never came back. And about how all of them were praying. And one day God would bring him back.

"You really believe that?" said Mr. English.

"Of course!" said Sarah Naomi.

CHAPTER 11

The Pelican's Story

TWO DAYS LATER the weather turned cold again. No big blizzard this time, but snow fell day after day, piling up and piling up.

Sarah Naomi couldn't help worrying about Mr. English. The old Heathe cabin was no place to live in now.

Twice she almost told Robbie she knew his secret. But she didn't. Mother never mentioned missing the rolls. Perhaps she never found out. But why didn't he just *ask* for the things? Mother and Father were always good to strangers.

This day Robbie was restless in school. He kept staring at the snowflakes that tumbled out of the sky all day. He seemed in a dreadful rush to get home after school. Wally and the sleigh were waiting at the door before Sarah had finished cleaning the brushes for Teacher. Robbie scolded her for keeping him waiting. At home he suddenly disappeared before supper.

"Where's that boy again?" Sarah heard Father exclaim.

Robbie came galloping up the hill from the creek sometime later. He never said a word when Father scolded him. At the supper table Sarah found him looking at her in a strange way.

When she ran upstairs for something he was there right at her heels. He closed her door and stood with his back against it. Just *staring* at her. It made her feel funny.

"What did you tell him?" he croaked after a bit.

She stared back. "What are you talking about?"

"It must have been you," he said. "When did you sneak after me to the Heathe cabin?"

Sarah grinned. "Oh, you mean Mr. English. It was at the quilting bee. I saw you sneaking away—with the rolls. So I ran after you. I heard voices and afterwards, when you had gone, I saw Mr. English. No, it was a couple days later."

Robbie made a choking sound. It wasn't a laugh, and it wasn't a groan. His hand fumbled in his pocket. He threw a crushed bit of paper at her. It landed *plop* at her feet. When she had opened it and smoothed it she read,

> Sorry, Pal. I find I can't face it after all. Just born with a yellow streak, I guess. Thanks anyway. It was a good try. And give my love— No, I guess we better skip that.

The note was signed "The Pelican, alias Jack English."

"But—but" said Sarah, bewildered. "What's Mr. English talking about?"

"Mr. English!" Robbie sounded scornful and sad too. "You really don't know yet who he is, do you?"

A crawly feeling ran up her spine. She shook her head.

"He's Keith, that's who!" Robbie's voice shook, he felt so bad.

Keith. Sarah's mouth opened. She clapped a hand to it, but no scream came. Keith. Keith John Scott—Jack English. Jack for John, English for Scott.

"What I'd like to know," said Robbie grimly, "is what you said that made him want to run away again."

"I never," said Sarah piteously. "I just—"

"Well, what is this *pelican* thing?"

"Sarah," came Mother's call that minute. "Where have you disappeared to? The dishes, remember?"

"Coming, Mother." Then she whispered. "Do we tell, Robbie?"

"No!" said Robbie. "Don't you dare! Not *anybody*."

"No," agreed Sarah slowly and sadly. "Oh, Robbie!" She was close to crying now.

For Father and Mother would feel dreadful if they knew that Keith had been so close—so *close*—and had gone away again. And yet—she felt as if she'd burst if she couldn't talk about it to someone.

Just before bedtime Robbie sneaked into her room again and they talked in whispers for a bit. He told her that Mr. Slocum brought Keith back on his last trip—the hurry-up trip Mrs. Slocum talked about! He bought cattle at the ranch where "Jack English" worked as cowhand. He'd expected Keith would go straight home, but Keith was too much ashamed to, or something. He moved into the cabin—to study the lay of the land, he said. And Robbie found him there one day. Robbie knew him almost the minute he saw him.

"And he was going to come home. I know he was. So what did you say to change his mind?" Robbie asked.

"Nothing. Really and truly. I just told him things—

about Kathleen and Herbie's wedding—and about Herbie going to be a minister. So then he wanted to know how come. And I told about the revival in summer and about all of us getting saved. Oh, Robbie, do you suppose that was it?"

Well, whatever it was, they couldn't do anything about it now. But they agreed that they had better keep quiet.

"Mother just simply couldn't bear it," whispered Sarah as Robbie was slipping from the room again.

Next morning Mr. Slocum was waiting beside the road for them. He looked as worried as they felt, and almost as sad.

"Well, Sarah Naomi, and what have you stirred up this time?" he asked, sounding almost fierce. "First you make me hunt up your brother—"

"I never!" said Sarah, astonished.

"You better take my word for it. That absent-loved-one prayer of yours. Sorta got under my skin, as you might say. Seein' as I was responsible for his goin' in the first place—"

"What?" said Robbie sharply.

"Didn't mean to say that," he muttered, looking uneasy. And *ashamed.*

Mr. Slocum, thought Sarah. Her memory skipped back to September. The wedding—someone saying something about Keith getting a "neighborly assist" when he ran away. *Mr. Slocum.*

"Well, if you must know," he was saying, "I used to tease Keith a bit. [Sarah could imagine!] About bein' under your old man's thumb. I suspected you was havin' ructions at home. He usta unload pretty freely when he was at our house. So, well, I just sorta—well, kept the fires stirred up, as you might say."

"And you kept coming to visit us after that, like a good friend!" said Robbie.

"Ever had a sore tooth, son? It hurts like all get out, but you can't stop bitin' it just the same. Well, there ye have it. My conscience kept botherin' me."

"You didn't act that way, Mr. Slocum," said Sarah.

"Didn't I? Well, you better take it from me," he said, "but in that blizzard—well, you tellin' about the prayer for the absent loved one— As I was sayin', it got under my skin. So I go to try an' persuade him to come back—"

"You knew all the time where he was?" gasped Sarah.

They stared at Mr. Slocum, and he grew redder and redder.

"Giddap, Wally," said Robbie.

And all the rest of the way to school Sarah and Robbie spoke only once.

"Oh, Robbie!" wailed Sarah in a tight whisper.

"Yeah," muttered Robbie.

Both of them thought of how Mother and Father prayed and waited for their boy—all those years and years! And they never knew if he was sick, or even if he was alive or not. But Mr. Slocum knew, and they thought he was their friend.

It was a good thing Christmas was so near. Miss Haliday handed out the parts for the Christmas program, and Sarah and Robbie were in two plays each. Rehearsals and decoration filled their school hours. Mother was sure that was what made Sarah so absentminded at home. So was Father. At first.

One evening Mr. Slocum came over. To see Coral and the calf, he said. But he and Father had a long talk in the barn. As soon as Father came into the house Sarah could tell: Father *knew.*

His face was white, but his voice kept calm. He needed both Sarah and Robbie in the barn right away, he said.

Mother was busy baking Christmas cookies. She didn't look up. "But supper's almost ready," she reminded them.

"We'll be right back," promised Father.

He took them all the way to the barn, and even then he closed the door carefully. As if Mother might hear in the house!

Mr. Slocum had told him *everything*, he said. He was worried about Keith's health. So he decided he'd better confess the whole thing, and perhaps they two could go and find Keith—and bring him home. They meant to leave tomorrow.

"I hear that the two of you have been giving his conscience a pretty bad time of late," said Father.

Sarah looked at Robbie. He looked back at her. Both of them had red faces. But Father was smiling faintly.

For a week or two they would be responsible for most of the chores again, he said. Stuart had to study for Christmas examinations right now.

"Will we tell Mother?" said Robbie soberly.

"No," said Father. He sounded very decided. "Not yet. I hope she'll forgive me— I dare not raise false hopes, in case—in case—" His adam's apple bobbed, but he didn't say in case of what.

Sarah felt that crawly feeling again, but this time it was like a band of ice creeping around her heart.

"What about Stuart?" said Robbie.

"Yes. He'll have to know. I'll tell him," Father said.

Father must have talked to Mother about the trip that night. She wasn't very happy about it at breakfasttime. She said she couldn't see why Mr. Slocum should have to go on one of his jaunts just at this time, and especially why he thought Father's advice would be needed in his business deals.

"I'm sorry to disappoint you," said Father, speaking sort of stiffly. "But I gave my word."

After that Mother said no more about it. But her silence was an unhappy thing. And they daren't tell her! The first chance Stuart got, he cornered Sarah and Robbie.

"You two!" he said. "Had to keep it to yourselves. Whatever for?"

"Because—because," said Sarah, "if I got talking about it at all I might not be able to stop. And we *couldn't* tell Mother."

"No," he agreed. "You couldn't tell Mother."

In the next week or so they got a couple of I-am-well-and-hope-you-are-the-same notes from Father. Then *nothing*. For eight days there wasn't a single word. But the week before Christmas a letter came. Mother was holding it tightly in her hands when Robbie and Sarah came home from school. She held it, and she walked back and forth, and her face looked sort of splendid. Like a lovely sunrise.

"Praise the Lord!" she whispered. "Oh, praise the Lord! Thank You, Lord Jesus!" Then she saw the two standing just inside the door, and she spread out her arms for them.

"Your brother Keith is coming home!" she said.

The letter was from *him*. It was a happy-sorry kind of

letter. But Father had added a few lines too. Mr. Slocum had thought of some places in Calgary where Keith might be. And at last they found him. He was sick when they found him, but now he was getting better every day.

"Best of all, Sheila, our boy has come back to his God," Father added.

Keith had written the news to Mother too. She read bits of the letter to Sarah and Robbie and Stuart. Most of it was sort of private though.

This was the biggest Christmas present of all! Others had come in the mail. Kathleen and Herbie sent Sarah some material for curtains and a skirt for her dressing table. Pink! It was going to be real nifty. Aunt Jane sent her a brush and comb and mirror set. In pink too! Linda

and her father sent a dozen books. So Christmas would have been exciting anyway.

But when Keith came in the door the day before Christmas, looking tall and thin and pale but smiling, Mother went straight to him. For a while nobody said a single word. He just held Mother as if he couldn't let her go again. The silence broke when Father blew his nose. It sounded like a trumpet!

"Welcome home, Son," he said huskily.

They did some singing before supper. But not much. Sarah hadn't known before that you could be too happy for singing, but you could. Father got down the old Bible then, and everyone knew what he was going to read:

> This my son was dead, and is alive again; he was lost and is found. And they began to be merry.

Mother stuffed the goose for tomorrow's dinner, and they talked. Once they began it was hard to stop. But this was Christmas Eve. Braeburn school was having its concert tonight. To Sarah's disappointment, Keith said he didn't feel up to going. And Mother almost stayed home too.

"I'll be here when you get back," Keith promised.

"You're sure?" Mother laughed a little, but she looked serious too.

"Very sure. Right now the Princess' claim on you is stronger than the Pelican's."

Robbie was on his way to the door. He swung around in a hurry. "What's this *pelican* thing?" he wanted to know.

"Secret," said Keith. "Between me and my little sister." And he winked at her.

My little sister. Sarah was almost dizzy with excitement. At school she whispered the important news to anyone who would listen. *"My big brother Keith has come home!"*

Braeburn school was like fairyland tonight. Colored stencils decorated all the blackboards. Balls and bells of green and red hung from the ceiling. Streamers twirled gaily overhead. And near the stage stood a tall evergreen decorated with cotton for snow, walnuts painted gold, and strings of popcorn. Colored candles burned on all the branches. The smell was lovely—woodsy as anything. Mr. Heathe sat close to the tree all evening to snip out a candle flame if it burned down too low.

Everybody had come. Fathers, mothers, big brothers and sisters, little ones who hadn't begun school, even tiny babies. The school desks were jammed. Everybody was there—except the Pelican.

Sarah Naomi knew why Keith chose that name. When she thought he was Mr. English she told him about the day she thought of running away from home—when she felt so lonesome—as lonesome as the pelican in the wilderness. Maybe Keith felt that way too.

But he wasn't alone anymore. He had a family now, and he had come back to God.

She looked over the sea of faces. Mr. Slocum was there. Because of him, Keith had run away—maybe. Because of him, Keith was home now. He paid for Father's trip, and he found out where Keith was staying and everything. She looked straight at him and smiled.

The Braeburn concert had begun. Sarah joined in the opening school song and sang from her heart.

Oh, joy to the world!